D&S VOL. 40

Fighter, Attack, Bomber, and Electronic War- Aircraft

# U.S. Aircraft & Armament of Operation Desert Storm

## in detail & scale

Bert Kinzey

KALMBACH BOOKS

Airlife Publishing Ltd.

England

## CONTRIBUTORS AND SOURCES:

Major Richard Cole, USAF
Major Charles Davenport, USAF
LT Fred Drummond, USN
Captain Dave Bennett, USA
Jim Rotramel
Dana Bell
Marty Isham
Jim Ivey

Don Linn
Anthony D. Chong
Paul Negri
Thomas M. Lore
Terry Love
Lloyd S. Jones
Ray Leader
Bud Colvin

Alan Toon
Flightleader
Grumman Aerospace
McDonnell Douglas
U. S. Air Force
U. S. Navy
U. S. Marines
Department of Defense

Most photographs in this publication are credited to their contributors. Photos with no credit indicated were taken by the author.

Cataloging-in-publication data

Kinzey, Bert.
    U.S. Aircraft & Armament of Operation
Desert Storm in detail & scale / by
Bert Kinzey.
        p.   cm. -- (D&S vol. 40)
    I. Airplanes, Military--United States--
Armed Forces--Aviation supplies and
stores--History--20th Century.
3. Persian Gulf War, 1991--Aerial
operations, American. 4. Projectiles,
Aerial--History--20th Century.
I. Title. II. Series.

[UG1243.K5     1993]
    358.4'183'097309050--dc20
                            93-20524
                            CIP

First published in Great Britain in 1992
by Airlife Publishing, Ltd.
7 St. John's Hill, Shrewsbury, SY1 1JE

British Library Cataloguing in Publication Data
        A catalogue record for this book
        is available from the British Library

ISBN: 1 85310 634 8

*Front cover: This A-7E was painted in a unique brown and tan camouflage scheme just after Operation Desert Storm. The words DESERT STORM were lettered across the top of the wings and on the fuel tanks. It was the CAG aircraft for VA-72 during the war, and it operated from the USS JOHN F. KENNEDY, CV-67, as part of Carrier Air Wing Three.         (Official U.S. Navy Photograph)*

*Rear cover: Desert Storm kill and mission markings on ten different types of aircraft illustrate how various squadrons represented the participation of their aircraft in the Gulf War. Overall views of these aircraft can be found on the front cover and on the pages of this book.*

# INTRODUCTION

*A pilot climbs into the cockpit of his F/A-18 Hornet aboard the aircraft carrier USS MIDWAY, CV-41, while the ship was deployed in the Persian Gulf during Operations Desert Shield and Desert Storm. This F/A-18 is armed with Sidewinder and Sparrow air-to-air missiles as well as its internal 20-mm cannon. The MIDWAY has since been decommissioned and taken out of service.*

*(Official U.S. Navy Photograph by CWO Ed Bailey)*

This volume in the Detail & Scale Series is being written in response to a very large number of requests. We have received numerous phone calls and letters asking for a book in this series on the U.S. aircraft and armament of Operation Desert Storm. During a visit to Washington, D.C., and a trip to the International Plastic Modelers Society's national conventions in St. Louis and Seattle, the author was approached time and time again about doing such a book. Almost everyone who contacted Detail & Scale made two very important points. First, they are far from pleased with most of the publications on Desert Storm that have been released so far. This is because many of these publications were rushed into print to make a quick profit off of the war. As a result, the accuracy and scope of those books often suffered considerably. Some had photographs and information from only one source, and there was often an obvious lack of original research. Military photographers who took the photographs were not technical experts, and the captions that they supplied with their photos often contained errors. In attempts to beat another publisher's book to the market, these obvious errors were often left uncorrected.

The second thing that the people who contacted the author wanted was a book that would specifically address the needs of scale modelers in building accurate replicas of the aircraft that participated in Desert Storm. They desired a book that was not rushed onto the shelves but was thoroughly researched through a number of sources. They wanted it to provide worthwhile

information about the aircraft and weapons that were used during the Gulf War. In addition to these requests, Detail & Scale was also approached by a number of pilots, flight crew and ground crew personnel, and other people directly involved with the war effort about doing this book. More important, some of these people offered direct and invaluable assistance in the book's preparation.

This is the fortieth title in the Detail & Scale Series, and in order to meet the requests that we have received for a book on Desert Storm, it must depart in several respects from the well known format established by the previous volumes. First, this title is not on a specific aircraft or ship, but it is about a considerable number of aircraft instead. This means that the aircraft illustrated between these covers are not depicted in the usual detail to show their cockpits, radars, avionics, weapons systems, landing gear, and other components. Almost all of the aircraft included in this publication have been treated separately in individual books in this series, and references to those volumes is made as appropriate. This book takes a brief look at each of the U.S. fighter, attack, bomber, and electronic warfare aircraft that played a major role in Operation Desert Storm. Information is provided on how each aircraft was used, what units participated, and what ordnance loads were typical for each of the aircraft. Photographs taken during and immediately after the Gulf War are included to illustrate the aircraft with the markings and external stores they carried in combat.

*The most successful aircraft during Operation Desert Storm was the F-111F. The sixty-six F-111Fs of the 48th Tactical Fighter Wing destroyed more targets from tanks to bridges, and from bunkers to hardened aircraft shelters, than any other aircraft in the war.*

*(Detail & Scale collection)*

The second section of this book takes a look at the primary weapons that were carried by these aircraft during the war. Laser guided and electro-optically guided smart bombs, air-to-ground missiles, air-to-air missiles, cluster bombs, the fuel air explosive bomb, and the various types of standard bombs are all included. ECM pods are also covered since they were often carried on Air Force aircraft. Photographs of each type of weapon or pod are provided along with a brief description of each. In many cases the photographs were actually taken during the war, but in some cases we have had to use better photographs that were taken when the armament was on display. An effort has been made to correct some of the misinformation that has been disseminated about these weapons in other publications and by the news media. This section is highlighted by exclusive photographs of the actual two GBU-28 "Deep Throat" bombs that were dropped on the deeply buried bunker complex north of Baghdad. These bombs were developed during the war and could penetrate over 100 feet into the earth.

One of the primary requests that we have received has been for information about the weapons carried by the aircraft. Therefore, the typical armament loads for each type of combat aircraft are discussed. It is not possible to cover every combination of external stores that were used on each aircraft, but the most common loadouts are included. This will allow modelers to accurately portray external stores on their models of Desert Storm aircraft. After looking at the explanation of weapons carried by a given aircraft, the reader can then turn to the armament section of this book for a detailed look at the appropriate ordnance for that particular aircraft.

We have limited our coverage to the fighter, attack, bomber, and electronic warfare aircraft that were used by the United States. Helicopters of various types, command and control aircraft such as the E-3A Sentry, E-2C Hawkeye, and E-8 Joint-STARS, the KC-135, KC-10, KC-130, and KA-6D tankers, and other various supporting aircraft all played vital roles, as did aircraft from other nations that formed the coalition. However, it is not possible to cover all of them in a book of this size.

In addition to photographic coverage, two drawings are also included for each weapon. In most cases these drawings were

done specifically for this publication by the well known aviation author and researcher, Dana Bell, using official Department of Defense drawings and photographs as references. In each case, the smaller drawing is in 1/72nd scale, and the larger drawing is in 1/48th scale. Providing the drawings in the two most popular modeling scales is intended to assist the modeler in scratch building ordnance that is not provided in kit form. The drawings can also be used to correct existing kit armament or for converting one type of ordnance to another. It is also important to note that in some cases, Dana has "rotated" the drawing so that a planform view of any wings or fins is visible. This will aid considerably when it comes to scratchbuilding weapons or modifying kit-provided ordnance for models. Lastly, we have provided some information about the colors of the weapons, but two points should be mentioned concerning these colors. First, some types of armament and ECM pods were not always painted the same color. Second, the olive drabs and grays used on many of the munitions varied considerably with respect to shading, so that it is often not possible to give a Federal Standard number that is consistent for all weapons or even a single type.

The information provided in the armament section will help the modeler choose the correct weapons for his model. Some ordnance is used only by the Air Force, while other weapons are carried only on Navy and Marine aircraft. For example, the Mk 82 Snakeye high drag bombs are no longer used by the Air Force, because they have been replaced by AIR (Air Inflatable Retard) bombs. So it would not be correct to put Snakeyes on a model of an F-16 used in Desert Storm. The Mk 83, 1000-pound bomb is used by the Navy and Marines, but not by the Air Force, so again a Mk 83, 1000-pound bomb should not be used on a model of an F-16 or any other Air Force aircraft. However, the M117, 750-pound bomb is used by the Air Force, but not the Navy or Marines. Points like these are covered in both the aircraft and armament sections of this book as appropriate.

Illustrating markings has never been a primary purpose of the Detail & Scale Series. Instead, that is the principle intent of our Colors & Markings Series. However, we have included some of the Gulf War markings in this publication. There are two reasons for this. First, these markings are such a distinctive and impor-

With its bomb racks empty, an A-6E from Carrier Air Wing Eight returns to the ROOSEVELT after a mission. ROOSEVELT operated two squadrons of Intruders during Desert Storm, and these included VA-36 and VA-65. She also operated two F/A-18 squadrons. The only other carrier to have two Intruder squadrons was RANGER, CV-61, but she did not embark any Hornet squadrons.

*(Official U.S. Navy photograph by PHC Denis Keske)*

tant part of the aircraft and Operation Desert Storm. Second, very little quality coverage of these markings has been published to date. Many of the photographs that are now generally available are the standard photos that have been provided to everyone by the Air Force, Navy, and Marines.

The modelers section also departs from our usual format. Obviously, it is not possible to have detailed kit reviews for all of the aircraft that are covered in this publication. It will be necessary for the modeler to check the Detail & Scale volume for the specific aircraft he is modeling to obtain in-depth kit reviews. In this book, we have taken each of the aircraft that is covered and have briefly discussed the best kits that are available in each of the popular modeling scales. We have polled knowledgeable modelers to get their opinions as to which are the best kits to use.

We have also covered the armament in our modelers section, including where the various weapons can be found in kit form. Notes are provided on how to convert one weapon to another to obtain a weapon which is not available in any kit.

To date, this is the only book about the Gulf War that is designed specifically to fill the needs of the modeler. With a look

at the actual aircraft and weapons that were used during the war, and with a review of the best model kits available, this book provides the modeler with invaluable information to assist him in building accurate scale models of the aircraft that made the headlines in Operation Desert Storm. The information and photographs that are included were compiled and assembled during hundreds of hours of research. Dozens of sources within the Air Force, Navy, and Marines were contacted as were many individuals. Trips were made to air bases and naval air stations by the author and Detail & Scale's contributing photographers to photograph the aircraft as they returned from the Persian Gulf. A special thanks is due Jim Rotramel for the information he provided about the various weapons. Major Dick Cole provided a considerable amount of assistance in the form of photographs, information, and suggestions. LT Fred Drummond, the only man with combat experiences in both the EA-6B Prowler and the EF-111A Raven, furnished photographs and invaluable information on those two aircraft. Other contributors helped in many ways, and most of their names are listed on page two. Detail & Scale and the author sincerely thank all of them.

**Left:** *When Operation Desert Shield ended and Desert Storm began, ground crews often expressed their feelings by writing messages on bombs that were destined for targets in Iraq or Kuwait. One such message can be seen in this photograph, while other messages are illustrated on page 40.* **(USAF)**

# AIRCRAFT

## F-15C EAGLE

*The F-15C Eagle was used by the Air Force to gain and maintain air supremacy over the Iraqi Air Force. This aircraft is from the 53rd Tactical Fighter Squadron of the 36th Tactical Fighter Wing which is home based at Bitburg Air Base, Germany. This unit is credited with seven confirmed air-to-air kills during Operation Desert Storm.* *(USAF)*

To gain and maintain air superiority over Iraq and Kuwait, the U.S. Air Force deployed F-15C Eagles to three air bases in Saudi Arabia and to Incirlik, Turkey. Official reports indicate that 120 Eagles participated in Operation Desert Storm, however, it is known that this number included at least two, if perhaps not a few more, two-seat F-15Ds. None were lost in combat or to non-combat reasons during Desert Shield or Desert Storm. These aircraft flew over 5,900 sorties while maintaining a ninety-four percent mission capable rate. This is eight percent higher than in peacetime. All sorties were air superiority missions, and no F-15Cs or -Ds delivered any ordnance against ground targets. The Eagles not only maintained air superiority, they provided true air supremacy that allowed other aircraft to perform their missions without interference from the Iraqi Air Force. All fixed wing air-to-air victories scored by the U.S. Air Force were made by the F-15C, and the Eagles, along with other fighters that performed the air superiority mission, were so effective that not one coalition aircraft was lost to enemy air action. The table on the next page provides information on all of the USAF F-15C squadrons that participated in Operation Desert Storm.

Air Force sources confirm thirty-six aerial kills were made by F-15Cs during the Gulf War. Most of these were scored with AIM-7F/-M Sparrow missiles, but AIM-9L/-M Sidewinders were also used. In one case, Captain Cesar Rodriguez of the 58th TFS, 33rd TFW, was given credit for a kill when the MiG-29 he was

flying against flew into the ground. No weapon was used for this kill which occurred on January 19. At the time, Captain Rodriguez was flying F-15C, 85-114.

Originally, Captain Steve Tate from the 1st TFW was given credit for the first air-to-air kill of the war. This remained "official" until September 6, 1991, when the Air Force issued Memorandum Number 401-M which stated: "Initial examination of available flight tracking information indicated that Captain Steve Tate, an F-15 pilot with the 1st Tactical Fighter Wing at Langley Air Force Base, VA, had scored the first aerial kill. However, closer examination of information on his downing of an Iraqi Mirage F.1 at 3:54 a.m. showed him to have shot down the fourth enemy aircraft in the four-week war."

The memorandum also stated, "Captain Jon B. Kelk, 32, assigned to the 33rd Tactical Fighter Wing, shot down an Iraqi MiG-29 at 3:10 a.m., Saudi Arabia time, January 17, just hours after the allied forces began bombing Iraq. Kelk's kill took place about forty-five minutes before what was originally reported as the first enemy aircraft shot down." The report went on to say, "Captain Robert E. Graeter, another F-15 pilot with the 33rd Tactical Fighter Wing, scored the second and third kills in Desert Storm. He is credited with downing two Iraqi Mirage F.1s at 3:24 a.m."

This revision concerning the first air-to-air victory of the war was determined by a U.S. Central Command review board while

*The 71st Tactical Fighter Squadron of the 1st Tactical Fighter Wing scored the fourth confirmed victory of the war when Captain Steve Tate shot down a Mirage F.1 while flying F-15C, 83-017. However, that was the only kill credited to that unit. This is one of the 1st TFW's F-15Cs at its base in Saudi Arabia.* *(USAF)*

*Fourteen confirmed victories are credited to the 33rd Tactical Fighter Wing from Eglin Air Force Base, Florida. This was the highest number of air-to-air kills scored by any unit.* (USAF)

studying the times as recorded by AWACS aircraft from the 552nd Airborne Warning and Control Wing from Tinker Air Force Base, Oklahoma. The Air Force stressed that the memorandum in no way detracted from the accomplishments of Captain Tate, but was issued only to correct the historical record.

In addition to their internal Vulcan cannon, F-15Cs carried a standard armament load of four AIM-7F/-Ms on their fuselage stations, and four AIM-9L/-Ms shoulder mounted on their underwing pylons. Three 600-gallon fuel tanks were also carried most of the time, with one being attached to the centerline station and one to each wing pylon.

Reports indicate that AIM-120A AMRAAMs (Advanced Medium Range Air-to-Air Missiles) were also available, and that they were actually carried by F-15Cs of the 33rd TFW late in the war. However, there was never any opportunity to use one of these missiles in combat. It appears that the AIM-120As were carried in place of the Sidewinders on the inboard pylon launch rails, but photographs also provide evidence that they were carried on the outboard rails as well.

It should also be noted that two squadrons from the Royal Saudi Air Force operated F-15Cs during the war. These were the 13th and 42nd Squadrons based at Dhahran. On January 24, a Saudi F-15C flown by Captain Al-Shamrani shot down two Iraqi F.1EQ-5 Mirages that were carrying Exocet missiles. They were reportedly heading for U.S. ships in the Persian Gulf. These kills were both scored with Sidewinder missiles. The Saudi's experienced one non-combat loss of an F-15C.

*The 32nd Tactical Fighter Group from Soesterberg Air Base, The Netherlands, also provided F-15Cs and pilots in support of the war effort. They worked with the 36th TFW, and often pilots from the two wings would fly aircraft assigned to the other wing. This is the commander's aircraft of the 32nd TFG. Note the name WOLF-HOUNDS painted on the nose. This unit operated out of Turkey during the war.* (USAF)

## F-15C EAGLE UNITS IN OPERATION DESERT STORM

| SQUADRON | WING | TAIL CODE | HOME BASE | OPERATING BASE |
|---|---|---|---|---|
| 27th TFS | 1st TFW | FF | Langley AFB, VA | Dhahran, SA |
| 71st TFS | 1st TFW | FF | Langley AFB, VA | Dhahran, SA |
| 32nd TFS | 32nd TFG | CR | Soesterberg AB, The Netherlands | Incirlik, Turkey |
| 58th TFS | 33rd TFW | EG | Eglin AFB, FL | Tabuk, SA |
| 53rd TFS | 36th TFW | BT | Bitburg AB, Germany | Al Kharj, SA |
| 525th TFS | 36th TFW | BT | Bitburg AB, Germany | Incirlik, Turkey |

# F-15E STRIKE EAGLE

*The 4th Tactical Fighter Wing (since redesignated the 4th Wing) from Seymour Johnson Air Force Base, North Carolina, provided all forty-eight F-15E Strike Eagles that were used in Operation Desert Storm. This photograph shows one of their aircraft armed and ready for a mission from Al Kharj Air Base, Saudi Arabia, during the war. It is armed with Rockeye cluster bombs and AIM-9M Sidewinder missiles.* *(Bennett via Davenport)*

At the time the United States began deploying forces in support of Operation Desert Shield, only one tactical fighter wing in the Air Force was operational with the F-15E Strike Eagle. That wing was the 4th TFW based at Seymour Johnson AFB, North Carolina, and only two of its squadrons had received all of their aircraft and were ready for combat. These were the Chiefs of 335th TFS and the Rockets of the 336th TFS. Forty-eight F-15Es, divided equally between these two squadrons, deployed to Al Kharj Air Base, Saudi Arabia, for Operation Desert Storm. Aircraft from both squadrons carried the 4th Tactical Fighter Wing's SJ tail code but could be distinguished from one another by their tail bands. The 335th TFS used a green band, while the tail band on aircraft from the 336th TFS was yellow. After the end of Desert Storm, the 4th Tactical Fighter Wing became the 4th Wing, and it now also operates KC-10 Extenders.

The "Mud Hens" flew approximately 2,200 missions during their combat debut while maintaining a 95.9 percent mission capable rate. This was eight percent higher than in peacetime. Primary targets included Scud missiles, command and control links, armor and other vehicles, airfield, and Iraqi convoys. Two were lost in combat, but there were no non-combat related losses. When they left Seymour Johnson, the aircraft were equipped with LANTIRN (Low-Altitude, Navigation-and-Targeting, Infrared for Night) navigation pods which were fitted to hardpoints under the aircraft's right engine inlet. Prior to the wing's departure for the Middle East, one of the companion targeting pods had arrived at Seymour Johnson AFB, but it had proved unreliable and was left behind. In December 1990, twenty-four of the targeting pods, which were still under development, were rushed to Saudi Arabia. This was only enough to equip half of the F-15Es, so when the Strike Eagles delivered laser guided bombs they worked in pairs. The lead aircraft would have the targeting pod attached under its left inlet and the navigation pod under the right inlet. The second aircraft in the pair had only the navigation pod. Since development and testing of

the targeting pods had not been completed, they were found to be less reliable than the older, but tried and true, Pave Tack system on the F-111F. However, their success rate was still higher than expected.

During Operation Desert Shield, an F-15E was photographed with four AIM-7F/-Ms on the conformal fuel tank (CFT) stations and four AIM-9L/-M Sidewinders on the wing pylon stations. However, it appears that this load, consisting only of air-to-air missiles, was not carried during the war. Before it was realized that the Iraqi Air Force was going to make a run for the border rather than stay and fight, two AIM-7F/-Ms were sometimes seen on the left CFT, while six Mk 20 Rockeyes were loaded on the right CFT. The Sparrows were soon deleted from the Strike Eagle's ordnance load, and all CFT stations were used for carrying ordnance to hit targets on the ground. For some time, the four AIM-9L/-M Sidewinders remained standard on the wing pylons, but this load was later reduced to two when the air threat continued to decrease to the point it became a non-factor.

When the F-15Es carried GBU-10C laser guided bombs, they

*The 4th TFW painted bomb symbols on its Strike Eagles to indicate missions flown during the war. Each bomb stood for five completed missions, so this F-15E, 87-183, completed at least forty-five missions.*

*Mk 82, 500-pound bombs are attached to the pylons of this Strike Eagle. F-15Es delivered both guided and standard bombs during the war and attacked targets ranging from tanks to Scud missiles.*
*(Bennett via Davenport)*

were attached to the front and rear bottom hardpoints on the conformal fuel tanks, meaning that four bombs were carried. Two or three 600-gallon fuel tanks were carried as necessary, but it seems that, more often than not, only two tanks were carried on the wing pylons, and the centerline station was left empty.

GBU-12D laser guided bombs were used for "tank plinking" during the later stages of the air campaign. As many as eight of these weapons were carried on the upper and lower, front and rear CFT stations.

Standard bombs and CBUs were also delivered by Strike Eagles, and they were seen attached to hardpoints on the con-

formal fuel tanks. Most common stores included Mk 82, 500-pound LDGP bombs, Mk 20 Rockeyes, and CBU-87 CEM (Combined Effects Munitions) cluster bombs.

F-15Es from the 335th Fighter Squadron of the 4th Wing were used again in the attacks against Iraqi surface-to-air missile sites during January 1993. This included the night attack on January 13 and the daylight mission on January 18. In spite of the bad weather that was encountered over the targets during the first attack, the F-15Es achieved an eighty percent accuracy rate with their laser guided bombs. This was the best of any type of aircraft used in these raids.

*This photograph is illustrative of the variety of weapons that the F-15E can carry. AIM-9M Sidewinder missiles are on the shoulder-mounted launch rails for use against enemy aircraft should they be encountered. A GBU-12B/B laser guided bomb hangs from the wing pylon. Unguided Mk 82, 500-pound air inflatable retard (AIR) bombs are attached to the hardpoints on the conformal fuel tank.* *(Detail & Scale collection)*

*This close-up shows details of the weapons pylons on an F-15E. The pylon under the wing is the same as that on other variants of the F-15, but there are three single and one long multi-station pylon on each conformal fuel pallet, and all are clearly illustrated in this view. Yet another pylon is under each intake. The one under the right intake carries a LANTIRN (Low Altitude, Navigation and Targeting, Infrared for Night) navigation pod, while the one under the left intake is for the similar LANTIRN targeting pod. The navigation pod can be seen in this photograph.*

*All forty-eight F-15Es traveled to Saudi Arabia with AAQ-13 Low Altitude, Navigation and Targeting, Infrared, for Night (LANTIRN) navigation pods attached to the right inlet station as shown here. Later, AAQ-14 targeting pods, which were still under development, arrived and were carried on the left inlet station. However, targeting pods were only available in sufficient quantity to equip about half of the F-15Es.*

# F-16 FIGHTING FALCON

*There were 249 F-16 Fighting Falcons deployed to the Middle East by the United States during Operation Desert Storm. Seventy-two of these were equipped with LANTIRN navigation pods as illustrated in this photograph. This pod, which can be seen attached to the intake, gave these seventy-two F-16s a limited night attack capability. An ALQ-131 deep ECM pod can be seen on the aircraft's centerline station. F-16s typically, but certainly not always, carried two external fuel tanks under the wings as shown here, while the center, and sometimes outer, wing stations were used for carrying ordnance. Sidewinders were habitually carried on the wing tips. The MY tail code on this F-16C indicates that it belongs to the 347th TFW which is based at Moody AFB, Georgia.* (USAF)

More F-16 Fighting Falcons were deployed to the Middle East for Operation Desert Storm than any other type of combat aircraft. Official numbers released by the Air Force state that 249 Falcons participated in the war. Whether this includes F-16C Wild Weasels flown by the 52nd TFW out of Incirlik, Turkey, is uncertain. Most of the force consisted of F-16Cs, but two Air National Guard squadrons with early production block F-16As were also on hand. Included in the total of 249 aircraft were a few two-seat F-16Ds as well. There were five combat losses of F-16s during the war, and three more were lost to non-combat related causes.

Although used in greater numbers than any other combat aircraft, the damage caused to the enemy by F-16s was minimal when compared to other aircraft types. As one Air Force official put it, "The lightweight fighter proved to be just that. It was the least effective aircraft in the war." There are two main reasons for this, and it is certainly not a reflection on the pilots and ground crews who flew and maintained the aircraft during the war.

First, the F-16 is indeed a small fighter with an airframe that is drag critical. It is limited in range and ordnance carrying ability when compared to larger fighters and attack aircraft. Second, the tactics that the F-16s were forced to use through most of the Gulf War also reduced their effectiveness. In order to keep them above deadly anti-aircraft artillery fire, F-16s were ordered to bomb from high altitudes, which meant that they usually maintained an altitude of at least 10,000 feet. Because there was little doubt about the outcome of the war, senior planners believed that it was prudent to protect American lives and aircraft by keeping them at these higher altitudes. With only one engine and far less armor protection, F-16s could not sustain the battle damage of the A-10 Warthog. The Falcon's avionics and bombing system was designed for low-level attacks and was not able to accurately deliver "dumb" bombs against point targets such as tanks, trucks, or artillery pieces from such high altitudes. Therefore, the effectiveness of the aircraft suffered. Without the ability to designate targets for smart weapons, F-16s delivered no laser guided bombs during the war.

At one point during Operation Desert Storm, F-16s were ordered to be on the ground by mid-afternoon so that the dust from their bombs could settle. This allowed F-111Fs and F-15Es to go out at night and more effectively destroy Iraqi tanks and other targets with laser guided bombs. They usually used GBU-12Ds for this mission that became known as "tank plinking."

Of the 249 Fighting Falcons that participated in the war, only seventy-two F-16Cs were equipped with LANTIRN pods, and these only had the navigation pod that was carried on the left chin station. Once the F-16C is fitted with the targeting pod, which will be carried on the right chin station, it will be able to self-designate for the delivery of laser guided bombs. However, the two LANTIRN pods will further limit the range of the drag critical airframe.

Two AIM-9L/-Ms were carried on the wing tip stations, and early in the war two additional Sidewinders were sometimes seen on the outboard wing stations. As the war progressed and the air threat diminished, these outboard pylons and their missiles were deleted, leaving only the Sidewinders on the wing tips. With very few exceptions, the inboard wing pylons were used to carry 370-gallon fuel tanks. The centerline hardpoint carried the ECM pod, and both ALQ-119 and ALQ-131 deep ECM pods were used. This left the center wing stations to carry the ordnance that was to be delivered to the Iraqis on the ground. Single Mk 84 bombs, Maverick missiles, and various cluster bombs were carried on these stations. For short range missions, triple ejector racks (TER) were fitted to each of the center wing pylons. Weapons loads carried on these two racks included six Mk 82, 500-pound bombs (three per rack) or four cluster bombs. In most cases, the CBUs were carried in the "slant-two" configuration, which means that one was attached to the lower and outboard stations on each TER. However, because they were smaller and lighter than other CBUs, six Mk 20 Rockeyes were sometimes loaded on the TERs. In a few instances, the fuel tanks were deleted, and four Mk 84, 2000-pound bombs were carried on the center and inboard wing pylons. Obviously, this load was used only on missions of very short range, even with the use of in-flight refueling.

*This F-16C is assigned to the 401st TFW, which is based at Torrejon Air Base, Spain. The 401st was one of several USAFE units that deployed aircraft to the Middle East.* **(USAF)**

*The 169th Tactical Fighter Group from the South Carolina Air National Guard was one of many Guard units to support Operations Desert Shield and Desert Storm. The unit's home base is McEntire ANGB. Note the ALQ-119 ECM pod on the centerline station.* **(Bennett via Davenport)**

The 174th TFW of the New York Air National Guard tried using their GPU-5, 30-mm gun pod one time during the war. It was carried on the centerline station, and the ALQ-119 long ECM pod was moved to the left center wing pylon. The right center wing pylon carried an AGM-65D Maverick missile. However, "The Boys from Syracuse" found that they could use bombs and CBUs to destroy targets more effectively and with less risk to themselves.

The F-16C Wild Weasels from the 52nd TFW usually carried AGM-88 HARM anti-radiation missiles on their center wing pylons. On a few occasions AGM-45 Shrike anti-radiation missiles were used instead of the HARMs. When anti-radiation missiles were not carried, Mk 82 or Mk 84 LDGP bombs were sometimes carried, while at other times CBU-58H or CBU-87 cluster bombs were loaded on the center wing pylons instead. Four Sidewinders were carried on the wing tip and outer wing stations, and the usual 370-gallon fuel tanks occupied the inboard hardpoints. An ALQ-131 deep ECM pod was carried on the centerline pylon.

One photograph showed an F-16C from the 388th TFW carrying four AIM-9L/-M Sidewinders on the wing tip and outer wing pylons. An ALQ-131 deep ECM pod was on the center left wing pylon, and external fuel tanks were attached to the centerline and inboard wing stations. The photograph did not reveal what, if anything, was on the center right wing pylon. This picture was taken early in Desert Shield, and there is no evidence to indicate that this pure air-to-air weapons load was used on F-16s during

Desert Storm.

Although no F-16 shot down an Iraqi aircraft during the Gulf War, an F-16C from the 33rd Fighter Squadron of the 363rd Fighter Wing scored the first combat kills made with the AIM-120A AMRAAM when hostilities in Iraq broke out again on December 27, 1992. On that date, an F-16C shot down a MiG-25 Foxbat. Then on January 17, 1993, another F-16C used an AMRAAM to destroy an Iraqi MiG-23 Flogger. These were also the first aerial kills made by U.S. Air Force F-16s in combat. Photographs of F-16Cs taken at that time showed two AIM-120A AMRAAMs loaded on the wing tip stations, while two AIM-9L/-M Sidewinders were carried on the outboard wing pylons. Fuel tanks were in position on the inboard wing stations, and an ALQ-119 long ECM pod was on the centerline station.

F-16Cs were also used to attack ground targets in the raids that occurred during January 1993. Again they were forced to use unguided gravity bombs from high altitude. Very bad weather also hampered the first mission, and the combination of these factors resulted in the Falcons missing most of the targets. Considering the fact that the F-16C's weapons delivery systems are designed for lower altitudes, this lack of success is understandable. However, if the planners insisted in using the higher altitude, area weapons such as cluster bombs would have been a better choice. The Pentagon has criticized CENTCOM on this point.

The following table provides a list of the F-16 units that participated in Operation Desert Storm.

## F-16 FIGHTING FALCON UNITS IN OPERATION DESERT STORM

| SQUADRON | WING | TAIL CODE | HOME BASE | DEPLOYMENT BASE |
|----------|------|-----------|-----------|-----------------|
| 10th TFS | 50th TFW | HR | Hahn AB, Germany | Al Dhafra, UAE |
| 23rd TFS | 52nd TFW | SP | Spangdahlem AB, The Netherlands | Incirlik, Turkey |
| 157th TFS | 169th TFW | * | McEntire ANGB, SC | Al Kharj, SA |
| 138th TFS | 174th TFW | NY | Hancock Field, NY | Al Kharj, SA |
| 69th TFS | 347th TFW | MY | Moody AFB, GA | Al Minhad, UAE |
| 17th TFS | 363rd TFW | SW | Shaw AFB, SC | Al Dhafra, UAE |
| 33rd TFS | 363rd TFW | SW | Shaw AFB, SC | Al Dhafra, UAE |
| 4th TFS | 388th TFW | HL | Hill AFB, UT | Al Minhad, UAE |
| 421st TFS | 388th TFW | HL | Hill AFB, UT | Al Minhad, UAE |
| 612th TFS | 401st TFW | TJ | Torrejon AB, Spain | Incirlik, Turkey |
| 614th TFS | 401st TFW | TJ | Torrejon AB, Spain | Doha, Qatar |

* The 169th TFW does not use tail codes. It is part of the South Carolina Air National Guard and has the words **SOUTH CAROLINA** painted in white on a blue/gray tail band.

# F-4G PHANTOM II (WILD WEASEL)

*The only combat version of the Phantom II to see action in Operation Desert Storm was the F-4G Wild Weasel air defense suppression aircraft. Two wings provided all of the F-4Gs used during the war, and both are illustrated in this photograph. The two aircraft in the foreground have WW tail codes, and this indicates that they are from the 35th Tactical Fighter Wing which is based at George AFB, California. The two aircraft in the background are from the 52nd TFW out of Spangdahlem Air Base, Germany, as indicated by their SP tail codes. Each of the aircraft is armed with four AGM-88 HARM anti-radiation missiles.* *(USAF)*

When Operation Desert Storm began, the mission with the highest priority was to gain air superiority so that coalition aircraft could carry out their strikes against Iraqi targets with as little opposition as possible. This not only included sweeping the skies of enemy aircraft, it also meant neutralizing the vast ground based air defense systems. At the beginning of the Gulf War, only the Soviet Union had a more complex and elaborate ground based air defense network than the Iraqis. While dedicated electronic jamming aircraft, internal electronic countermeasures systems, and external ECM pods provided some of the protection, many aircraft actively sought out and destroyed the radar systems that controlled the surface-to-air missiles. In many cases, these were standard fighter and attack aircraft like the F/A-18 Hornet, the A-6 Intruder, and the A-7 Corsair II, which were armed with AGM-88 HARM anti-radiation missiles and other weapons to destroy the radars and missile sites. One aircraft, the F-4G Wild Weasel, was specifically designed to perform this job.

F-4Gs were converted from existing F-4E airframes, and fitted with low, mid, and high-band sensors to detect enemy radar emissions. Electronics and computers in the aircraft analyze the threat and determine the type of radar and missile system being encountered. These aid the electronics warfare officer in determining which poses the greatest danger. The F-4G can then attack the missile site to destroy its radar and other compo-

nents. While destroying the radar and/or missile site may be desirable, since this prevents it from ever being used again, the mission can also be successful even if the Wild Weasel does not actually destroy the target. Merely suppressing the site is usually sufficient to protect the other aircraft in the strike package so that they can attack their targets. In order to survive, radar operators at guided missile batteries often turn their radars on and off repetitiously (called blinking) or leave them off altogether. This limits, and sometimes prevents, anti-radiation missiles from homing in on them. But it also severely degrades or even eliminates that surface-to-air missile unit's ability to track and engage targets. In short, the presence of the F-4G Wild Weasel left the Iraqis with the choice of turning their radars off and being ineffective, or turning them on and being destroyed. Either way, the radar guided surface-to-air missile systems were suppressed and neutralized.

Forty-eight F-4Gs flew missions out of Sheikh Isa, Bahrain, while approximately twenty more operated with F-16Cs from Incirlik, Turkey. They flew more than 2,800 sorties while maintaining a mission capable rate of 87.5 percent. Other published sources have stated that no F-4Gs were lost during Operation Desert Storm, but the fact is that one F-4G was lost on January 19 in combat. Fortunately, both crewmen were rescued. This is quite remarkable considering the Weasel's very dangerous mission. No F-4Gs were lost to non-combat causes.

*The 35th TFW, as well as some other units, painted out some of their standard markings while operating in the Middle East. Note that the TAC badge on the tail of this aircraft has been covered with dark gray. More difficult to see is the light gray that was used to paint over the wing badge on the intake. The ALQ-184 ECM pod with its longer gondola is visible in this photograph. It is located in the forward left Sparrow bay.* *(USAF)*

*An F-4G from the 52nd TFW moves in to refuel from a tanker during Operation Desert Storm. It is carrying four AGM-88 HARM anti-radiation missiles.* *(USAF)*

*When an AGM-88 HARM missile is carried on the outboard wing pylons of an F-4G, the pylon must be angled slightly outward to provide clearance between the missile's wings and the main landing gear doors.* *(Lore)*

For self-defense, the F-4Gs carried two AIM-7F Sparrow missiles in their aft fuselage missile bays. The right forward bay was empty, and an ECM pod was carried in the left forward missile bay. Aircraft from the 35th TFW carried the ALQ-184 ECM pod, while those from the 52nd TFW used the ALQ-131 deep pod instead. A 600-gallon fuel tank was standard for the centerline station. While the F-4Gs sometimes carried an AGM-88 HARM on each of their four wing pylons, the more common load consisted of two HARMs and two 370-gallon fuel tanks. The HARMs were carried on the inboard wing stations, while the tanks were carried on the outboard hardpoints. Even when these two tanks were carried, the centerline tank remained in place. For a short time during the war, AGM-45 Shrike anti-radiation missiles replaced the HARMs. It has also been reported that F-4Gs of the

52nd TFW, while operating out of Incirlik, expended a few Maverick missiles during the war. If this is true, the Mavericks would have been carried on the inboard wing pylons. The total number of Mavericks fired by these aircraft probably did not exceed fifty.

In late 1992, Iraq started moving air defense missile batteries into the northern and southern "no-fly" zones imposed by the United Nations, and it became clear that military action would again be necessary to knock out these units. F-4Gs from the 52nd TFW participated in the strikes that began on January 17, 1993. Whenever the Iraqi radars locked on to coalition aircraft during the days that followed, the Wild Weasels were on hand to destroy or suppress the SAM sites with their HARM missiles.

Three squadrons from two wings flew the F-4Gs during Desert Storm. The units are shown in this table:

## F-4G WILD WEASEL SQUADRONS IN OPERATIONS DESERT SHIELD & DESERT STORM

| SQUADRON | WING | TAIL CODE | HOME BASE | DEPLOYMENT BASE |
|---|---|---|---|---|
| 23rd TFS | 52nd TFW | SP | Spangdahlem AB, Germany | Incirlik, Turkey |
| 81st TFS | 52nd TFW | SP | Spangdahlem AB, Germany | Sheikh Isa, Bahrain |
| 561st TFS | 35th TFW | WW | George AFB, California | Sheikh Isa, Bahrain |

# RF-4C PHANTOM II

RF-4Cs from the 106th Tactical Reconnaissance Squadron of the 117th Tactical Reconnaissance Wing are shown at their home base in Birmingham, Alabama, shortly after returning from the Middle East. The 106th TRS is part of the Alabama Air National Guard.

Although the RF-4C is not actually a fighter or even a combat aircraft, it is the reconnaissance version of one of the most famous fighter designs in history. Therefore, we have elected to include its use during Desert Shield and Desert Storm in this publication.

RF-4Cs were among the oldest aircraft to participate in the Gulf War, and most were veterans of the Vietnam conflict. Shortly after the war, the author visited the 106th Tactical Reconnaissance Squadron at Birmingham, Alabama, to gather information for this book. As photographs were being taken of one of the aircraft that participated in Operation Desert Storm, one of the pilots pointed out patches in the skin of the aircraft. The patches covered holes made by flack in the skies over Vietnam more than twenty years earlier. Today, the few remaining RF-4Cs are the only tactical reconnaissance assets left in the Air Force's inventory.

The first RF-4Cs to deploy to the Gulf were six aircraft from the 106th TRS of the 117th TRW. This unit is part of the Alabama Air National Guard. Two of these aircraft had the KS-127 camera with a 66-inch focal length lens. As these aircraft flew just south of the borders of Iraq and Kuwait, their KS-127 cameras took detailed photographs of enemy installations, equipment, and troop movements as far as fifty miles away. The only externally visible feature that distinguishes these specially equipped aircraft from standard RF-4Cs is the addition of two aiming devices attached to the insides of the rear canopy rails.

While supporting Operation Desert Shield, the 106th TRS was tasked with 570 missions, and they maintained a perfect 100 percent mission capable rate by flying all 570 missions. Then crews from the Nevada Air National Guard's 192nd TRS relieved those from the Alabama ANG. They brought one of their own RF-4Cs and another from the Mississippi ANG as replacement aircraft, but otherwise continued to operate four of the six RF-4Cs from the 106th TRS. By that time, one of the original six Phantoms deployed by the 106th TRS had been lost in a non-combat related crash in October 1990 during Desert Shield. The

An RF-4C moves in on a tanker during a mission near the Iraqi border. An ALQ-131 deep ECM pod is carried on the right inboard wing pylon. These pods were common on RF-4Cs during Operation Desert Shield and Desert Storm, and were also seen on the left inboard pylon instead of the right. *(USAF)*

The only external evidence that an RF-4C is equipped with the KS-127, 66-inch focal length camera is the addition of two aiming devices on the rails of the rear canopy. Only two RF-4Cs carried this amazing camera during the war, but they provided excellent photographic coverage of what the Iraqis were doing along the border during Operation Desert Shield.

*Some of the art painted on the RF-4Cs of the 117th TRS is illustrated in this photograph. This is the left side of the nose section of 65-843 which is the squadron commander's aircraft for the 106th TRS. It has a colorful shark's mouth and eyes, although some of the other aircraft had low-visibility gray colors instead. A cartoon drawing of an RF-4C with a Confederate soldier is just above the air conditioning intake, and the words RECCE REBELS are lettered just above it. Three small camels are painted at the base of the inlet ramp, but the forward one is almost covered by the boarding ladder. These black camels each have white marks indicating missions flown. The forward and middle camels each have five marks, while the rear camel has four. This indicates that the aircraft flew fourteen missions during Desert Shield and Desert Storm.*

crews from the Nevada Air National Guard flew 412 missions. A second RF-4C was lost in a non-combat related crash after Operation Desert Storm was over, but none of the aircraft were lost to combat or non-combat causes during the war itself.

Two regular Air Force squadrons also flew RF-4Cs during Operation Desert Storm. These included the 12th TRS of the 67th TRW and the 38th TRS of the 126th TRW.

The standard configuration for F-4Cs during Desert Shield and Desert Storm was two 370-gallon fuel tanks carried on the outboard wing pylons. The centerline station was usually left

empty, as was one of the two inboard wing pylons. The other inboard wing station carried an ECM pod. Both the ALQ-119 long pod and the ALQ-131 deep pod were used. One photograph of a 106th TRS RF-4C showed an ALQ-131 deep pod on the left inboard station, and on the right inboard pylon was a shoulder-mounted launch rail with a Sidewinder missile. A pilot from the squadron explained to the author that they never could have fired the missile, but the Iraqis didn't know that!

The following RF-4C units participated in Desert Shield and Desert Storm:

## RF-4C PHANTOM SQUADRONS IN OPERATIONS DESERT SHIELD AND DESERT STORM

| SQUADRON | WING | TAIL CODE | HOME BASE | DEPLOYMENT BASE |
|----------|------|-----------|-----------|-----------------|
| 12th TRS | 67th TRW | BA | Bergstrom AFB, Texas | Sheikh Isa, Bahrain |
| 38th TRS | 26th TRW | ZR | Zweibrucken AB, Germany | Incirlik, Turkey |
| 106th TRS | 117th TRW | BH | Birmingham, Alabama | Sheikh Isa, Bahrain |

One aircraft from the Nevada Air National Guard's 192nd TRS, 152nd TRG, and another aircraft from the Mississippi Air National Guard's 153rd TRS, 186th TRG, also participated in the war.

*Very subdued art like this was painted on several RF-4Cs of the 106th TRS after personnel from the 192nd TRS of the Nevada Air National Guard rotated in to relieve the crews from Alabama. Although it is difficult to see because of the subdued colors that were used, there is a palm tree at the center of the art with a map of Nevada on its trunk. The words 412 UNIT SORTIES are written inside the map.*

*The camera laden nose section of this RF-4C has been opened up for maintenance. Like almost all RF-4Cs used in Desert Shield and Desert Storm, this aircraft is a veteran of the war in Vietnam, and still has patches in its skin that were made by flak more than twenty years ago.*

# F-111E/-F AARDVARK

*Ground crew personnel scurry around an F-111F from the 48th TFW as they perform last minute checks prior to a mission. The aircraft is armed with two GBU-24A, 2000-pound, laser guided bombs. Note that the wing pylons which are not being used to carry stores for this mission have been removed. The F-111F was far and away the most effective and successful aircraft used during the war.*

*(USAF)*

Both the F-111E and F-111F flew combat missions in Operation Desert Storm. The 79th Tactical Fighter Squadron of the 20th Tactical Fighter Wing flew twenty F-111Es from Incirlik, Turkey, and suffered no combat or non-combat losses. These aircraft have UH tail codes indicating their home base of Upper Heyford, United Kingdom. None of the F-111Es that had received modernized avionics systems shortly before the outbreak of the war participated in Operation Desert Storm, and without the precision guided munition capabilities of the F-111F, the F-111Es that did participate only delivered conventional unguided ordnance. Four Mk 84, 2000-pound bombs were carried singly on pylons, and up to eight Mk 82, 500-pound bombs were carried on bomb release units (BRU). These were usually loaded in a slant-four configuration, meaning that the two lower and two outboard stations on each BRU was loaded with a Mk 82, while the two inboard stations remained empty.

Cluster bomb units were also delivered by F-111Es, and the most common load was either four CBU-87s or CBU-89s mounted singly on the pylons. For all missions, an ALQ-131 shallow ECM pod was carried on the aft fuselage station.

A very strong case can be made that the F-111F was the most successful aircraft in the war. During Desert Storm, the only operational combat wing with F-111Fs was the 48th "Statue of Liberty" Tactical Fighter Wing at Lakenheath AB, England. The wing's four squadrons that participated in the war were:

| SQUADRON | TAIL BAND | NAME |
| --- | --- | --- |
| 492nd TFS | Blue | Justice |
| 493rd TFS | Yellow | Freedom |
| 494th TFS | Red | Liberty |
| 495th TFS | Green | Independence |

Aircraft from all of these squadrons carried the LN tail code of the 48th TFW.

After flying 2,417 sorties without a loss from Tiaf, Saudi Arabia, the 48th TFW provided extensive documentation of their successes against the Iraqis. They dropped 5,576 bombs weighing 3,650 tons, and out of the approximately 8,000 precision

guided munitions dropped by all U.S. Air Force aircraft, 4,666, or well over half, were delivered by the sixty-six F-111Fs. Their results were spectacular. They completely destroyed 2,203 targets. This included confirmed direct hits on 920 tanks, with another five to six hundred probably destroyed. A total of 252 artillery pieces of all types, 67 troop and munitions assembly areas, 245 hardened aircraft shelters, 113 bunkers, 13 runways, 4 aircraft in the open, 13 hangars, 19 warehouses, 158 buildings, 23 logistics sites, 9 lines of communications, 25 SAM/AAA sites, 11 Scud sites, 5 pumping stations, 4 mine entrances, 32 chemical facilities, 9 towers, 2 ships, and 12 bridges (with another 52 seriously damaged) were all confirmed destroyed by these sixty-six aircraft.

F-111Fs were the only aircraft to participate in the Gulf War that were then certified to deliver the GBU-15 electro-optically guided bomb, and they were chosen to knock out the manifolds that were dumping oil into the Persian Gulf. F-111Fs dropped all seventy GBU-15s as well as the only two GBU-28 Paveway III laser guided bombs used during Operation Desert Storm. The GBU-28 dropped by the 495th TFS squadron commander's aircraft, 70-2391, scored a direct hit on a deep command bunker at Taji Air Base just north of Baghdad. It was one of three such bunkers where Saddam Hussein reportedly spent most of the war. Plans were made to destroy the other two bunkers in downtown Baghdad the following night, but the Iraqis agreed to meet all demands and resolutions of the United Nations before that mission could be flown. Only one GBU-28 was carried by each aircraft, and was loaded to the left outboard pylon. To help balance the aircraft, a single Mk 84, 2000-pound bomb was carried on the right outboard pylon.

Another mission flown by the F-111Fs that should be noted was one flown against Tallil airfield in southeastern Iraq. The leader's bombs scored a direct hit on an ammunition storage area and set off the largest man-made, non-nuclear explosion ever detected by a Defense Support Program missile warning satellite. Smoke from the explosion rose over 30,000 feet into the air, and because of the blast and smoke, only the leader's wingman, who had already dropped his bombs before the explosion occurred, was able to deliver his weapons. General Schawarzkopf reported the event to the media, although he did not point out that it was the venerable old F-111F that had flown the mission.

On the opening night of the war a few F-111Fs carried two AIM-9P-3 Sidewinders on the shoulder stations of their wing pylons. The use of the AIM-9P-3 was dictated by the clearance problems of the launch rails which did not permit use of the AIM-9L/-M with its larger wing span. After that first night, F-111Fs did not carry any Sidewinders.

When configured to deliver GBU-15 electro-optically guided bombs, the airborne-television, special-type, AXQ-14 data-link pod was mounted on the aft fuselage station, and the ALQ-131 shallow ECM pod was located on the forward fuselage station on the Pave Tack cradle. The Pave Tack pod itself was rotated into the bomb bay. Only two GBU-15s were carried at a time, and these were loaded on the outboard pylons. Often, the GBU-15s were dropped by one aircraft and guided by a second aircraft which carried the data link pod. This was how the bombs that knocked out the manifolds were guided, with the weapons systems officer in the controlling aircraft flying well outside the ground based defenses.

When laser guided bombs or unguided weapons were delivered, the ALQ-131 shallow ECM pod was carried on the aft fuselage station, and the airborne-visual, special type, AVQ-26 Pave Tack infrared laser designator pod was rotated out of its position within the specially modified bomb bay doors.

Up to four pylon-mounted GBU-10, -12, or -24 laser guided bombs were carried. If only two were carried on a mission, they were loaded on the outboard pylons, while the inboard pylons were left empty and were sometimes removed. In periods of bad weather, the outboard pylons were loaded with two GBU-10s or GBU-24s, while standard Mk 84, 2000-pound bombs were carried on the inboard pylons. If the weather cleared, the laser guided bombs were dropped with pinpoint accuracy. If it didn't, the two Mk 84s were dropped on area targets. In some cases, GBU-10s were loaded on the inboard pylons and the Mk 84s were attached to the outboard stations.

GBU-12Ds were used in "tank plinking" operations at night with great success. On one raid, twenty F-111Fs carrying eighty GBU-12Ds destroyed seventy-seven tanks. Thought was given

to having B-52Gs loaded with GBU-12Ds fly along with an F-111F. In addition to guiding its own bombs, the F-111F would designate targets for the bombs carried by the B-52Gs. However, Iraq almost ran out of tanks, and the war ended before this could be put into practice.

This table indicates the number of laser guided bombs dropped by the sixty-six F-111Fs:

| BOMB TYPE | NUMBER DROPPED |
|-----------|----------------|
| GBU-10E | 469 |
| GBU-10J | 389 |
| GBU-12D | 2,542 |
| GBU-24 | 270 |
| GBU-24A | 924 |
| GBU-28 | 2 |

F-111Fs also delivered a considerable amount of conventional ordnance to include 530 CBU-87s and 212 CBU-89 cluster bomb units. These cluster bombs were loaded singly on the four pylons. At least a few Mk 82, 500-pound bombs were also delivered early in the war, and it appears that these were carried on two bomb release units (BRU) fully loaded with a total of twelve bombs.

As this is written, the F-111Fs are being transferred to the 27th Fighter Wing at Cannon AFB, New Mexico, and the 48th Fighter Wing is being re-equipped with only two squadrons of F-15E Strike Eagles. The F-111 is old, but it can carry a heavier load faster and further, and deliver it as accurately as any other fighter-bomber in the world today. It was much maligned by the ignorant media and irresponsible politicians when it entered service a quarter of a century ago. But in spite of rapidly advancing technology and the passage of so many years, it still has capabilities today that cannot be found in any other aircraft. Even now it still seems that the F-111F does not get a fair shake. There is strong evidence that damage caused by F-111Fs during Operation Desert Storm was credited to other newer weapons systems by the Air Force in order to make them look better than they actually were. This is difficult to understand, since the newer Air Force aircraft, particularly the F-117A Night Hawk and the F-15E Strike Eagle performed quite well in their own right.

*It is the Pave Tack system that makes the F-111F so successful, and the F-111F is the only version of the Aardvark that has this system. This photograph shows the Pave Tack pod mounted in the bomb bay of an F-111F.* (Detail & Scale collection)

*This is the imagery seen through the Pave Tack system of an F-111F as the aircraft attacked a hardened aircraft shelter. Runways and taxiways are visible in the photograph. Smoke can be seen pouring from shelters that have been hit by other aircraft in the lower right hand corner of the photograph.* (USAF)

# EF-111A RAVEN

EF-111A, 66-030, awaits its next mission at Tiaf Air Base, Saudi Arabia. Mission markers can be seen under the cockpit.

(Drummond)

A total of eighteen EF-111A Ravens flew over nine-hundred sorties in support of coalition air strikes in Iraq and Kuwait. EF-111As from the 390th Electronic Combat Squadron of the 366th Tactical Fighter Wing based at Mountain Home Air Force Base, Idaho, flew missions from Tiaf Air Base, Saudi Arabia, during the war. Other Ravens from the 42nd Electronic Combat Squadron at Upper Heyford, England, operated from Incirlik, Turkey. One EF-111A, 66-0023, was lost in a non-combat related accident on February 14, and both crewmen were killed. Although unarmed, the Ravens made the skies safer for other aircraft by jamming enemy radar systems, thereby degrading the Iraqi's ability to acquire and track allied aircraft.

One of the most unusual incidents of Operation Desert Storm involved EF-111A, 66-016, on the opening night of the war. Known as "Sweet Sixteen" to many in the 390th ECS, this aircraft was crewed by Captain Jim Denton and Captain Brent Brandon for a mission in the H-2 area of Iraq. They were number two of a two-ship formation of EF-111s that were escorting F-15E Strike Eagles. The supporting E-3 Sentry AWACS aircraft warned the Ravens of approaching enemy fighters. As the Iraqi aircraft closed in on 66-016, Captain Denton made a "combat descent" where the nose of the aircraft is pointed down to thirty degrees below the horizon, then the automatic terrain following radar levels the plane out at one thousand feet above the ground. To

fool the guidance systems of any air-to-air missiles that might be launched against them, the crew released chaff and flares from their aircraft. The Iraqi pilots followed the Raven in its dive, but one of them could not pull out in time. He flew into the ground and his aircraft exploded. Meanwhile, two F-15Cs had been vectored toward the enemy aircraft, and one of the Eagles fired an AIM-7 Sparrow air-to-air missile just prior to the explosion. Evidence indicates that the Iraqi fighter flew into the ground and crashed before being hit with the AIM-7, but the F-15C was given credit for the kill.

In another case that occurred two days later on January 19, Captain Cesar Rodriguez, while flying an F-15C Eagle, was given credit for an aerial victory when he caused an Iraqi pilot to crash into the ground while maneuvering against him. One officer who flew with the 390th ECS during the war explained to the author that for the same reasons, he thought that Captains Denton and Brandon and their EF-111A should have been given credit for the kill in this case. When the author approached a senior Air Force official at the Pentagon about this incident, he agreed that by all rights, the EF-111A should have received official credit for the kill. But he stated, "The Air Force certainly is not going to credit an unarmed aircraft with an aerial victory for obvious reasons, particularly when it may well have been the first kill of the war."

*This is the wing commander's EF-111A Raven from the 366th Tactical Fighter Wing as it appeared in February 1991 at Tiaf Air Base, Saudi Arabia. The aircraft is named SPIRIT OF IDAHO, and is EF-111A, 66-014. A close-up of the mission markings can be found on the rear cover.*

*(Detail & Scale collection)*

EF-111A, 66-049, is shown on March 6, 1991, as it flew the last EF-111 mission over Iraq. Along with two F-15Cs, the Raven escorted two RF-4Cs on a recon mission over central Iraq. The RF-4Cs can be seen in the background as they refuel from a KC-135 prior to entering Iraqi airspace. *(Drummond)*

This marking was painted on the inlet ramps of 390th ECS EF-111As during Operation Desert Shield. *(Drummond)*

Once Desert Storm began, this marking was added. It was usually placed on the nose section of the aircraft just forward of the mission markings. *(Drummond)*

A Raven takes on fuel from a KC-135 during a mission in February 1991. The refueling took place over north central Saudi Arabia prior to a combat mission in Iraq. *(Drummond)*

# F-117A NIGHTHAWK

*The F-117A Nighthawk received more publicity than any other aircraft in the war, and it was indeed very successful. None of the aircraft were lost, nor did they receive any damage as they attacked high priority targets in heavily defended areas.* **(USAF)**

Receiving more media coverage during the war than any other type of aircraft was the F-117A Nighthawk. Although the news reporters often confused the F-117A stealth fighter with the B-2 stealth bomber, the success achieved by the forty-two F-117As certainly merited a considerable amount of attention by the media. Only the F-111F compiled a better record during Desert Storm.

But a lot of the media attention was based on hype generated by the Air Force itself. Many so called and self-appointed experts had been very critical of the F-117A prior to the war, and the Air Force cannot be blamed for wanting to publicize a more positive image of the stealth fighter based on its performance in Desert Storm. While there is some evidence that the claims about the number of targets destroyed by the Nighthawk were stretched somewhat by the Air Force, the fact remains that these stealth fighters delivered over 2,000 tons of laser guided bombs against the most heavily defended, high value targets in Iraq without

receiving a scratch. In fact, no F-117As were lost to combat or non-combat causes throughout their deployment to the Middle East. Because they could not see the Nighthawk on their radars, the Iraqis began to call it "The Ghost."

During Operation Desert Storm, the only combat wing that was equipped with the F-117A was the 37th TFW, which was based at Tonapah Test Range Airfield, Nevada. Aircraft and crews from that wing's 415th and 416th Tactical Fighter Squadrons flew 1,271 sorties and accumulated over 6,900 hours of flying time. All of these missions were flown at night from Khamis Mushait Air Base, Saudi Arabia. Targets included command and control facilities, bunker complexes, bridges, and other types of targets that were often in close proximity to civilians. The precision delivery capabilities of the Nighthawk kept the loss of civilian lives to a minimum.

All of the weapons delivered by the F-117A were laser guided bombs that were carried in pairs inside the weapons bay. The

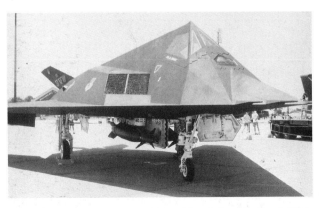

*Weapons are carried in an internal bomb bay on the F-117A. They are attached to a rack or "trapeze." In this photograph, the bomb bay doors are open, and the two laser guided bombs can be seen hanging down on the lowered bomb racks.* **(Ivey)**

*An F-117 is moved out of its protective hangar at Mushait Air Base, Saudi Arabia.* **(USAF)**

*The Nighthawk form is unmistakable in the air as well as on the ground. This photograph was taken during the flight over to Saudi Arabia.* (USAF)

*A parabrake is used to slow the Nighthawk during its landing roll.* (USAF)

types carried included GBU-10 and GBU-12 Paveway II as well as GBU-27 Paveway III laser guided bombs.

After the Gulf War was over, the F-117As were transferred from the 37th TFW to the 49th Fighter Wing at Holloman AFB, New Mexico. Some of the "Black Jets" remained in the Middle East, and they participated in the attacks on Iraqi surface-to-air missile sites and airfields during January 1993. During the first raid, which took place on January 13, the F-117s had problems with the cloud cover over the targets, and this caused some of their laser guided bombs to break lock on the target. One Nighthawk pilot could not even see his target through the clouds, so he did not drop his bombs. However, a follow-up attack in better weather proved to be more successful.

*With its refueling receptacle open, an F-117A moves in on a tanker to refuel during the long flight to Saudi Arabia.* (USAF)

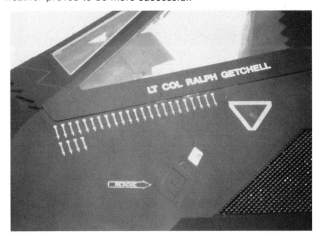

*Silhouettes of laser guided bombs that are painted below the canopy rail attest to the missions flown by this F-117A during the war.* (Isham)

# F-14 TOMCAT

*The CAG's (Commander of the Air Group) F-14 Tomcat from VF-154 is shown here on the flight deck of the USS INDEPENDENCE during Operation Desert Shield. Although most Tomcats are still in the tactical paint scheme with subdued low visibility markings, a lot of color is starting to reappear on the fighters. This is true for regular squadron aircraft as well as those in CAG markings. Note that this F-14 is armed with a Sidewinder and a Sparrow missile on the wing glove pylon, but no Phoenix missiles are carried.* *(DOD)*

A total of 109 F-14 Tomcats participated in Desert Storm, but because their areas of operations had very little enemy air activity, and also because the Iraqi Air Force decided to run for the border, the F-14s did not get to experience any real playing time in air-to-air combat. In fact, the only air-to-air kill scored by a Tomcat during Operation Desert Storm was against an Mi-8 Hip helicopter. F-14A, 162603, scored this victory on February 6, using an AIM-9M Sidewinder. This Tomcat was from VF-1's Wolfpack and had a modex of 103. Like all aircraft assigned to Carrier Air Wing Three aboard the USS RANGER, CV-61, it carried an NE tail code. The pilot for this mission was LT Stuart Broce, and the RIO was the squadron's CO, CDR Ron McElraft. An F-14A+ from VF-103 was the only Tomcat lost during the war.

Typical missions for Tomcats during the Gulf War were flying fleet defense missions called combat air patrols (CAP) and providing fighter escort for strike packages. It is known that F-14s from VF-2 used their internal 20-mm cannon to strafe Iraqi naval vessels, and there may have been other instances when Tomcats strafed ground targets. Although F-14s are now being equipped to carry bombs, none were used to deliver ordnance against ground targets during Operation Desert Storm.

Another important mission performed by some Tomcats was that of airborne tactical reconnaissance. One of the two F-14 squadrons in a carrier air wing have specially equipped Tomcats that can carry and operate the tactical air reconnaissance pod system (TARPS). This system includes a large pod that is fitted under the fuselage of the aircraft, and it is controlled from a special panel in the rear cockpit. TARPS is another example of a system that had been criticized in the media before the war, but worked extremely well in the real world. There are no dedicated reconnaissance aircraft in the Navy inventory any more, so the TARPS equipped F-14s have to provide all of the tactical airborne reconnaissance. However, these Tomcats retain all of the weapons and fighting capability of standard Tomcats.

Tomcats typically carried their "standard" 2-2-2 mix of air-to-air missiles. This load includes two AIM-7F/-M Sparrows on the lower station of each wing glove pylon, two AIM-9L/-M Sidewinders on the shoulder station of each glove pylon, and two AIM-54C Phoenix missiles on the forward two fuselage stations. Early in the war, some units evidently added to this load by carrying Sparrows or Phoenix missiles on the aft fuselage stations. Later the AIM-54Cs were replaced with one or two Sparrows on the forward fuselage stations, and the aft stations were

*VF-74 and VF-103 were assigned to Carrier Air Wing Seventeen aboard USS SARATOGA, CV-60, and they flew F-14A+ Tomcats during Desert Shield and Desert Storm. In the photograph at left, two Tomcats are already in position on catapults one and two, while others are preparing to move forward for their turns to launch. At right, an F-14A+ from VF-74 is about to touch down on the carrier after a mission.* *(Both DOD)*

*Tomcats also flew reconnaissance missions during the Gulf War. Personnel from VF-84 are shown here moving a Tactical Airborne Reconnaissance Pod System (TARPS) to one of the squadron's F-14s. VF-84 was embarked aboard USS THEODORE ROOSE-VELT during Operation Desert Storm.*           *(Official U.S. Navy Photograph by PHC Denis Keske)*

left empty. Two 265-gallon fuel tanks were standard, and were attached to the hardpoints on the engine nacelles.

In December 1992, the USS KITTY HAWK, CV-63, was operating off the coast of Somalia in support of the U.S. forces that were in that country to aid in the distribution of food to the starving population. By early January 1993, she had been moved to the Persian Gulf, and Carrier Air Wing Fifteen operated from her decks during the attacks on Iraqi missile batteries that had been moved into the "no-fly" zones. F-14 squadrons VF-51 (Screaming Eagles) and VF-111 (Sundowners) flew escort for the strike aircraft. Photographs indicate that their armament load was the standard 2-2-2 mix of missiles described above.

The following F-14 Tomcat squadrons participated in Operations Desert Shield and Desert Storm:

## F-14 TOMCAT SQUADRONS IN OPERATIONS DESERT SHIELD AND DESERT STORM

| SQUADRON | AIR WING | CARRIER | MODEX | TAIL CODE | SQUADRON NAME | NOTES |
|----------|----------|---------|-------|-----------|---------------|-------|
| VF-142 | SEVEN | EISENHOWER | 1XX | AG | Ghostriders | 1, 2 |
| VF-143 | SEVEN | EISENHOWER | 2XX | AG | 'Pukin' Dogs | 1, 2 |
| VF-21 | FOURTEEN | INDEPENDENCE | 2XX | NK | Freelancers | 1 |
| VF-154 | FOURTEEN | INDEPENDENCE | 1XX | NK | Black Knights | 1 |
| VF-1 | TWO | RANGER | 1XX | NE | Wolfpack | |
| VF-2 | TWO | RANGER | 2XX | NE | Bounty Hunters | |
| VF-14 | THREE | KENNEDY | 1XX | AC | Tophatters | |
| VF-32 | THREE | KENNEDY | 2XX | AC | Swordsmen | |
| VF-33 | ONE | AMERICA | 2XX | AB | Starfighters | |
| VF-102 | ONE | AMERICA | 1XX | AB | Diamondbacks | |
| VF-41 | EIGHT | ROOSEVELT | 1XX | AJ | Black Aces | |
| VF-84 | EIGHT | ROOSEVELT | 2XX | AJ | Jolly Rogers | |
| VF-74 | SEVENTEEN | SARATOGA | 1XX | AA | Be-Devilers | 2 |
| VF-103 | SEVENTEEN | SARATOGA | 2XX | AA | Sluggers | 2 |

Notes:

1. These units and carriers participated in Operation Desert Shield and were relieved on station prior to the start of Operation Desert Storm.

2. These units flew the F-14A+ variant of the Tomcat. This variant has since been redesignated F-14B, and it differs from the F-14A mainly in that it has the more powerful General Electric F110-GE-400 turbofan engines. F-14As have Pratt & Whitney TF30-P-412A engines.

The other carrier to participate in Operation Desert Storm was the USS MIDWAY, CV-41. It did not operate F-14s in its air wing due to limited overhead in its hangar bays. The USS MIDWAY has since been decommissioned and taken out of service.

# F/A-18 HORNET

*A pilot climbs into his F/A-18 Hornet in preparation for a mission from the USS THEODORE ROOSEVELT, CVN-71. VFA-15 and VFA-87 were the two F/A-18 squadrons that operated from the ROOSEVELT during Desert Storm and Operation Provide Comfort which followed.* (Official U.S. Navy photograph by PHC Denis Keske)

A total of 167 U.S. F/A-18 Hornets participated in Operation Desert Storm. Eighty-nine of these were flown by nine Navy squadrons, and seven USMC squadrons operated the other seventy-eight. Additionally, thirty-four Canadian CF-18s and crews from four different units flew in support of the coalition's air campaign. Reportedly, no more than twenty-six Canadian Hornets were in theater at any one time.

Some of the criticisms aimed at the Air Force's F-16 were also directed at the Hornet. Primary among these was its lack of range, and even the F/A-18's strongest supporters admit that the aircraft's short legs remain a problem. However, the Hornet can carry a heavier payload further than the F-16, and it appears to be more survivable in part because it has two engines instead of one. The F/A-18 also had better weapons delivery capabilities than the Falcon.

On January 17, while attacking an Iraqi airfield with Mk 84, 2000-pound bombs, two F/A-18Cs, 163502 and 163508, shot down two MiG-21 Fishbeds. These two Hornets were assigned to the Sunliners of VFA-81, one of the two F/A-18 squadrons that were part of Carrier Air Wing Seventeen aboard the USS SARATOGA. F/A-18C, 163508, was flown by LCDR Mark Fox, who shot down one of the two MiG-21s with an AIM-9M Sidewinder, while the other was piloted by LT Nick Mongillo. LT Mongillo used an AIM-7M Sparrow to destroy the other Fishbed. The two Hornets then resumed their attack on the airfield with the rest of their strike force. These two kills would remain the only Navy victories over Iraqi fixed-wing aircraft during the war.

Hornets carried a wide variety of external loads during the war, but AIM-9L/-M Sidewinders were standard for the wing tip stations except for Marine F/A-18Ds when they acted as fast forward air control (Fast FAC) aircraft. Most of the time, the centerline station was occupied with a 330-gallon fuel tank.

During most daylight missions, the fuselage stations carried AIM-7F/-M Sparrow missiles. These were supplemented with one or two additional Sparrows on inboard wing pylons whenever the Hornet was performing a strictly air-to-air mission such as combat air patrol or fighter escort. For night ground attack missions, the AIM-7 on the left fuselage station was often

replaced with an AAS-38 forward looking infrared (FLIR) pod. ASQ-173 laser spot tracker/strike camera (LST/SCAM) pods were carried on the right fuselage station when needed.

As many as four AGM-88 HARM anti-radiation missiles were carried on wing pylons for the SAM suppression mission. Fuel tanks were substituted on one or both of the inboard pylons if necessary to provide extra unrefueled range. One unofficial report also stated that Hornets used AGM-45 Shrike anti-radiation missiles as well. However, official Navy records do not show any Shrikes being fired by U.S. Navy aircraft during the war.

Mk 82, 83, and 84 standard bombs were delivered by Hornets, but the Mk 83, 1000-pound bomb appears to have been the one used most often by F/A-18s. In other references, Mk 83s, which are used only by the Navy and Marines, have been confused with both the smaller Mk 82 and the larger Mk 84. To carry six Mk 83s, horizontal ejector racks (HER) were attached to the two inboard pylons, and each carried two bombs. The other two 1000-pound bombs were loaded singly to the outboard pylons. A load of four Mk 83s was carried simply by loading them singly to the four wing pylons. Yet another combination was to carry a single Mk 83 on the two outboard pylons, a third on the centerline station, and fuel tanks on the two inboard pylons.

When the larger and heavier Mk 84, 2000-pound bombs were carried, the maximum load was four. These were loaded singly on the four wing pylons. When more range was needed, one or both of the bombs on the inboard pylons were replaced with fuel tanks. Mk 82, 500-pound bombs were carried singly or in multiples on horizontal ejector racks and multiple ejector racks (MER). When loaded singly or on HERs, these bombs were carried on any of the five weapons stations, however, it appears that MERs were only carried on the wing pylons. Rockeye cluster bombs were also carried in these same configurations, except MERs were not used to deliver these weapons. They were either loaded singly or in pairs on HERs.

Up to two AGM-62 Walleyes were carried, and these were usually loaded on the outboard wing stations. Fuel tanks were carried on the inboard pylons, and the AAW-7 data link pod for the Walleyes was attached to the centerline hardpoint. ADM-141 tactical air-launched decoys were also carried by Hornets, and up to six were loaded at any one time. These were carried on HERs on the inboard pylons and were mounted singly on the outboard stations.

Some reports have also indicated that F/A-18Cs were used to deliver laser guided bombs to include GBU-10E, GBU-12D, and GBU-16B bombs as well as the AGM-123 Skipper. Other sources state that the Marine Hornets also fired Maverick missiles, dropped Mk 77 napalm to ignite oil in Iraqi defensive trenches, and employed BLU-72 fuel air explosive bombs to detonate minefields.

Marine squadron VFMA (AW)-121 flew the night attack version of the F/A-18D in the Fast FAC role. This variant has the back seat control column and throttles replaced with controls and displays similar to those found in the F-15E. These aircraft carried weapons loads not seen on other Hornets. For self defense, a single AIM-7F/-M Sparrow was mounted on the right fuselage station, but no Sidewinders were carried on the wing tips. An AAR-50 Thermal Imaging Navigation Set (TINS) was carried on the left fuselage station. For long range missions, fuel tanks were attached to the two inboard wing stations. The outboard wing pylons carried HERs, and a LAU-10 rocket pod with four 5-inch rockets was attached to the outboard station of each of these HERs. For shorter range missions, the fuel tanks on the inboard stations were replaced with HERs, each of which was loaded with two Mk 82, 500-pound LDGP bombs. In this case, a centerline tank was carried, but the HERs and the rocket pod configuration for the outboard wing pylons remained the same.

During Operation Desert Storm, the Navy lost two Hornets in combat action and another to non-combat related causes. The Marine Corps lost two of their F/A-18s, both to non-combat related causes.

When the United States, Great Britain, and France launched strikes against Iraq in January 1993, two F/A-18C squadrons from Carrier Air Wing Fifteen participated in the action. These included the Chargers of VFA-27, and the Warhawks of VFA-97. Carrier Air Wing Fifteen aircraft carried an NL tail code. Modex numbers for VFA-27 were in the 300 series, while those of VFA-97 were in the 400 series. During the initial strikes on January 13, these Hornets met with limited success due to the fact that they were forced to drop unguided bombs from high altitudes in very bad weather.

Information about the Navy and Marine F/A-18 squadrons that participated in the Gulf War is summarized in the following table.

## U.S. F/A-18 HORNET SQUADRONS IN OPERATIONS DESERT SHIELD & DESERT STORM

### U.S. NAVY

| SQUADRON | AIR WING | CARRIER | MODEX | TAIL CODE | SQUADRON NAME | NOTES |
|----------|----------|---------|-------|-----------|---------------|-------|
| VFA-25 | FOURTEEN | INDEPENDENCE | 4XX | NK | Fist of the Fleet | 1, 2 |
| VFA-113 | FOURTEEN | INDEPENDENCE | 3XX | NK | Stingers | 1, 2 |
| VFA-131 | SEVEN | EISENHOWER | 4XX | AG | Wildcats | 1, 2 |
| VFA-136 | SEVEN | EISENHOWER | 3XX | AG | Knighthawks | 1, 2 |
| VFA-82 | ONE | AMERICA | 3XX | AB | Marauders | 2 |
| VFA-86 | ONE | AMERICA | 4XX | AB | Sidewinders | 2 |
| VFA-81 | SEVENTEEN | SARATOGA | 4XX | AA | Sunliners | 2 |
| VFA-83 | SEVENTEEN | SARATOGA | 3XX | AA | Rampagers | 2 |
| VFA-15 | EIGHT | ROOSEVELT | 3XX | AJ | Valions | 3 |
| VFA-87 | EIGHT | ROOSEVELT | 4XX | AJ | Golden Warriors | 3 |
| VFA-151 | FIVE | MIDWAY | 2XX | NF | Vigilantes | 3 |
| VFA-192 | FIVE | MIDWAY | 3XX | NF | Golden Dragons | 3 |
| VFA-195 | FIVE | MIDWAY | 1XX | NF | Dambusters | 3 |

### U.S. MARINE CORPS (5)

| SQUADRON | TAIL CODE | SQUADRON NAME | HOME BASE | NOTES |
|----------|-----------|---------------|-----------|-------|
| VMFA (AW)-121 | VK | Green Knights | El Toro, California | 4 |
| VMFA-212 | WD | Lancers | Kaneohe Bay, Hawaii | 2 |
| VMFA-232 | WT | Red Devils | Kaneohe Bay, Hawaii | 2 |
| VMFA-235 | DB | Death Angels | Kaneohe Bay, Hawaii | 2 |
| VMFA-314 | DR | Black Knights | El Toro, California | 3 |
| VMFA-333 | DN | Shamrocks | Beaufort, North Carolina | 3 |
| VMFA-451 | VM | Warlords | Beaufort, North Carolina | 3 |

Notes:

1. These units only participated in Operation Desert Shield
2. Indicates F/A-18C
3. Indicates F/A-18A
4. Indicates F/A-18D
5. All Marine Hornet squadrons operated from Sheikh Isa Air Base, Bahrain, during Operation Desert Storm.

# A-6E INTRUDER

*An A-6E taxis across the flight deck of the USS SARATOGA, CV-60, as the ship operates in the Red Sea. VA-35 was the Intruder squadron embarked in SARATOGA during Desert Shield and Desert Storm. (Official U.S. Navy photograph by CWO Ed Bailey)*

Eleven A-6E Intruder squadrons provided much of the Navy and Marine night attack capability against Iraq. Nine Navy squadrons with a total of ninety-five A-6Es operated from the six carriers, while the two Marine units, with an additional twenty Intruders, flew their missions from Sheikh Isa, Bahrain. Two other Navy squadrons, VA-34 and VA-195 participated in Desert Shield only. All of these aircraft had the Target Recognition and Attack Multi-sensor (TRAM) turret under the nose to acquire targets and guide PGMs to destroy them. Some of them had received the System Weapon Improvement Program (SWIP), which allowed them to employ the AGM-88 HARM, AGM-65 Maverick, AGM-84E SLAM, and AIM-120A AMRAAM missiles. Other SWIP improvements included J52-P-408/9 engines, digital controls and displays, an advanced radar, night attack navigation system (NANAS), a wide-angle head-up display, additional chaff and flare provisions, and dedicated air-to-air weapons stations. During the war, the Navy lost four of its Intruders in combat and another to non-combat related causes. The Marines operated their A-6Es without loss.

A-6Es carried a wide variety of ordnance in many different and almost imaginative loading configurations. Basically, the centerline station was used to carry a 300-gallon fuel tank, while the weapons were carried on the four wing stations. When necessary, additional 300-gallon fuel tanks were also carried on one or more of the wing pylons.

GBU-10E, GBU-12D, and GBU-16B laser guided bombs were delivered by Intruders, and these were mounted singly on the wing pylons. Two or four of the weapons were loaded depending on the target requirements and the range of the mission. When only two weapons were carried, they were mounted on the inboard or outboard pylons on each side, and the pylons not used were either left empty or fitted with external fuel tanks.

AGM-123A Skipper IIs were also used by A-6Es. It appears

that no more than two of these weapons were carried at any one time, and quite often only one was loaded. For example, Skippers were carried in mixed loads with Mk 20 Rockeyes and Mk 82, 500-pound LDGP bombs, for the armed surface reconnaissance mission. Two Mk 20s were carried on the forward and rear lower stations of a MER that was attached to one of the outboard pylons, while two Mk 82s were loaded in the same manner on a MER that was fitted to the other outboard pylon. The AGM-123A was loaded to one of the inboard pylons, and the other inboard station was used for an additional external fuel tank. For anti-armor missions, a load consisting of two GBU-12Ds on the outboard pylons, a single AGM-123A Skipper on one of the inboard stations, and fuel tanks on the other outboard pylon and the centerline station was sometimes used. A typical load for anti-ship missions included two Mk 20 Rockeyes attached to the lower front and rear positions on a MER that was carried on the left outboard pylon. A single GBU-12D laser guided bomb was loaded on the right outboard pylon. External fuel tanks were on the other three stations. Another configuration included six Mk 83, 1000-pound bombs that were carried in threes on MERs that were loaded on the outboard pylons. Because of the length of the Mk 83s, they were attached to the forward shoulder and rear lower positions of the MER. GBU-12Ds were carried singly on the inboard pylons, and the usual fuel tank was on the centerline station.

Loads consisting of standard gravity bombs and/or Rockeyes were also delivered by Intruders. As many as twelve Mk 82 LDGP or Snakeye 500-pound bombs were seen loaded on two MERs that were attached to either the inboard or outboard pylons. These twelve bombs were sometimes mixed with twelve Rockeyes that were carried on additional MERs that were loaded on the other two wing pylons. Up to ten Mk 83, 1000-pound bombs were carried, again loaded on MERs. However, it should be noted that at most only three of these weapons can be loaded on a MER at any one time. The usual configuration is two Mk 83s on

*A-6E, 162195, was assigned to VA-75 aboard the USS JOHN F. KENNEDY, CV-67, during Operation Desert Storm. It is shown here upon its return to the squadron's home base of Oceana Naval Air Station, Virginia, after the war. At left is an overall view of the aircraft that shows an AGM-88 HARM under the left wing of the aircraft. At right is a close-up of the mission markings that were painted on the nose of this Intruder.*

*(Both Ivey)*

the forward shoulder stations and one on the lower aft station. If only two Mk 83s are carried on a MER, one is usually attached to the forward outboard position, and the other is on the lower rear position. Single Mk 83s were also attached directly to the wing pylons. Up to four Mk 84, 2000-pound bombs were also carried on A-6Es, and these were loaded singly on the wing stations. Different types of weapons were also carried in mixed loads. For example, two Mk 83, 1000-pound bombs were sometimes loaded on the inboard stations and were mixed with twelve Mk 82, 500-pound bombs or twelve Mk 20 Rockeyes that were loaded on MERs and carried on the outboard stations.

For the air defense suppression mission, up to four HARMs were carried on the wing pylons, and it has been reported that AGM-62 Walleyes were delivered by Intruders. They also employed the ADM-141 Tactical Air Launched Decoy and laid sea mines. Marine Intruders dropped Mk 77 napalm to ignite oil in Iraqi defensive trenches, and they may have used some rocket

pods as well. Reports that Intruders also used the AGM-45 Shrike anti-radiation missile appear to be false, however, Intruders from VA-75 made the first combat launches of the Standoff Land Attack Missile (SLAM). Only seven of these missiles were used during the war.

A-6Es also served as aerial tankers for other carrier aircraft. When performing this mission, they carried a "buddy" refueling store on their centerline stations and 300-gallon fuel tanks on all four wing stations.

During the strikes against Iraq that were carried out in January 1993, Intruders once again were in the action. These aircraft were flown by the Knight Riders of VA-52, the Intruder squadron from Carrier Air Wing Fifteen aboard the USS KITTY HAWK. Their aircraft carried an NL tail code and had modex numbers in the 5XX series.

The following Navy and Marine Intruder squadrons participated in Operations Desert Shield and Desert Storm.

## A-6E INTRUDER SQUADRONS IN OPERATIONS DESERT SHIELD & DESERT STORM

| SQUADRON | AIR WING | CARRIER | MODEX | TAIL CODE | SQUADRON NAME | NOTES |
|----------|----------|---------|-------|-----------|---------------|-------|
| VA-34 | SEVEN | EISENHOWER | 5XX | AG | Blue Blasters | 1, 2 |
| VA-196 | FOURTEEN | INDEPENDENCE | 5XX | NK | Main Battery | 1, 3 |
| VA-35 | SEVENTEEN | SARATOGA | 5XX | AA | Black Panthers | 3 |
| VA-36 | EIGHT | ROOSEVELT | 53X | AJ | Roadrunners | 2 |
| VA-65 | EIGHT | ROOSEVELT | 50X | AJ | Tigers | 2 |
| VA-75 | THREE | KENNEDY | 5XX | AC | Sunday Punchers | 3, 4 |
| VA-85 | ONE | AMERICA | 5XX | AB | Black Falcons | 3 |
| VA-115 | FIVE | MIDWAY | 5XX | NF | Eagles | 2 |
| VA-185 | FIVE | MIDWAY | 4XX | NF | Nighthawks | 3 |
| VA-145 | TWO | RANGER | 5XX | NE | Swordsmen | 3, 4 |
| VA-155 | TWO | RANGER | 4XX | NE | Silver Foxes | 3, 4 |

## U.S. MARINE CORPS (5)

| SQUADRON | TAIL CODE | SQUADRON NAME | HOME BASE | NOTES |
|----------|-----------|---------------|-----------|-------|
| VMA (AW)-224 | WK | Bengals | Cherry Point, North Carolina | 2 |
| VMA (AW)-533 | ED | Hawks | Cherry Point, North Carolina | 2 |

Notes:
1. Participated in Operation Desert Shield only
2. Squadron did not have any KA-6D tankers assigned
3. Squadron aircraft included KA-6D tankers
4. Squadron aircraft had SWIP improvements
5. Marine squadrons operated from Sheikh Isa Air Base, Bahrain.

# EA-6B PROWLER

*The Grumman EA-6B Prowler provided electronic jamming support during the war. Here an EA-6B from VAQ-132 taxis among parked aircraft on the flight deck of the USS SARATOGA. Unlike the EF-111A, the Prowler also delivered weapons against the enemy. Note the HARM missile under the left wing pylon (to the right in the photograph).* (DOD)

The EA-6B Prowler flew its first combat missions over twenty years ago in Vietnam. Throughout that war, the raids on Libya, and in Operation Desert Storm, the Prowler has performed a dangerous mission admirably, and no EA-6B has ever been lost in combat. Unlike its EF-111A counterpart in the Air Force, Prowlers are armed, and do attack surface-to-air missile units as well as jam them with electronic countermeasures. However, the only weapon carried by EA-6Bs during Operation Desert Storm was the AGM-88 HARM, and no more than two of these anti-radiation missiles were ever carried at a time. HARM-capable Prowlers are the Improved CAPability (ICAP-2) variant, and all of the EA-6Bs used during the Gulf War were this type.

Six Navy squadrons flew twenty-seven Prowlers during Operation Desert Storm. Information about these units, as well as two others that participated only in Operation Desert Shield, is summarized in the table on the next page. Marine squadron VMAQ-2 deployed with twelve Prowlers to Sheikh Isa Air Base,

Bahrain, to provide electronic jamming support for Marine aircraft. VMAQ-2 is home based at Cherry Point, North Carolina. Their aircraft carry a CY tail code, and the squadron's name is Playboys.

As stated above, Prowlers often carried one or two AGM-88 HARM anti-radiation missiles during the Gulf War. The only two other external stores loaded on the EA-6Bs were ALQ-99 electronic countermeasures (ECM) pods and 300-gallon fuel tanks. HARMs were carried on the wing pylons, but not on the centerline station. The ALQ-99 ECM pods were seen on all five stations, while the 300-gallon fuel tanks were carried on the centerline station and on the inboard wing pylons. The loading of these three types of stores seemed to cover almost every possible combination, and it would appear that the individual units decided what store would go on each pylon. The following table includes examples of loadings carried on EA-6Bs during Operation Desert Storm.

## EA-6B PROWLER LOADING CONFIGURATIONS

| SQUADRON(S) | LEFT OUTBOARD | LEFT INBOARD | CENTERLINE | RIGHT INBOARD | RIGHT OUTBOARD |
|---|---|---|---|---|---|
| VAQ-130 | ALQ-99 | Fuel Tank | ALQ-99 | AGM-88 | AGM-88 |
| VAQ-130 | ALQ-99 | Fuel Tank | ALQ-99 | AGM-88 | ALQ-99 |
| VAQ-130 & -136 | AGM-88 | Fuel Tank | ALQ-99 | AGM-88 | ALQ-99 |
| VAQ-132 | ALQ-99 | AGM-88 | Fuel Tank | ALQ-99 | ALQ-99 |
| VAQ-132 | AGM-88 | Fuel Tank | ALQ-99 | Fuel Tank | ALQ-99 |
| VAQ-131 & -141 | AGM-88 | Fuel Tank | ALQ-99 | ALQ-99 | AGM-88 |
| VAQ-141 | AGM-88 | Fuel Tank | ALQ-99 | Fuel Tank | AGM-88 |
| VMAQ-2 | AGM-88 | Fuel Tank | ALQ-99 | Fuel Tank | ALQ-99 |
| VMAQ-2 | ALQ-99 | Fuel Tank | ALQ-99 | ALQ-99 | ALQ-99 |

*This EA-6B is from VAQ-130, which was assigned to Carrier Air Wing Three and the USS JOHN F. KENNEDY, CV-67, during Operation Desert Storm. It is shown inbound on a mission early in the war. Note the HARM anti-radiation missile on the inboard wing pylon. Although not visible in the photograph, an external fuel tank is on the left inboard pylon, and jamming pods are on the two outboard pylons as well as the centerline station.*

*(VAQ-130)*

## U.S. NAVY EA-6B UNITS IN OPERATIONS DESERT SHIELD AND DESERT STORM

| SQUADRON | AIR WING | CARRIER | TAIL CODE | MODEX | SQUADRON NAME |
|----------|----------|---------|-----------|-------|---------------|
| VAQ-139* | FOURTEEN | INDEPENDENCE | NK | 6XX | Cougars |
| VAQ-140* | SEVEN | EISENHOWER | AG | 62X | Patriots |
| VAQ-130 | THREE | KENNEDY | AC | 62X | Zappers |
| VAQ-131 | TWO | RANGER | NE | 6XX | Lancers |
| VAQ-132 | SEVENTEEN | SARATOGA | AA | 6XX | Scorpions |
| VAQ-136 | FIVE | MIDWAY | NF | 6XX | Gauntlets |
| VAQ-137 | ONE | AMERICA | AB | 62X | Rooks |
| VAQ-141 | EIGHT | ROOSEVELT | AJ | 62X | Shadowhawks |

Notes:

Squadrons marked with a * participated only in Operation Desert Shield.

The Garudas of VAQ-134 flew Prowlers in support of the strikes against Iraq during January 1993. These aircraft were part of Carrier Air Wing Fifteen aboard the USS KITTY HAWK. They carried an NL tail code and a modex in the 6XX series.

*EA-6B, 162934, was flown by the Scorpions of VAQ-132 during Operation Desert Storm. This squadron was part of Carrier Air Wing Seventeen aboard USS SARATOGA, and these two photographs of the Prowler were taken shortly after it returned from the war. Note the HARM anti-radiation missile on the inboard wing pylon in the overall view shown at left. A scorpion, indicative of the squadron's nickname, is painted high on the rudder. At right is a close-up of the mission markings on the nose of this aircraft. They illustrate HARM launches against radar installations.*

*(Both Chong)*

# A-7E CORSAIR II

*The Navy said farewell to the A-7 Corsair II during the Gulf War. Only two squadrons, VA-46 and VA-72 participated in the combat, and these were assigned to Carrier Air Wing Three aboard KENNEDY. This is one of VA-72's A-7Es, and it was photographed on a training mission during Desert Shield. Small practice bombs are attached to the multiple ejector rack (MER) under the wing.*
*(Official U.S. Navy photograph by CDR John "Lites" Leenhouts)*

Only two squadrons of A-7E Corsair IIs participated in Operation Desert Storm, and these were the last two A-7E units in Navy service. Both were part of Carrier Air Wing Three aboard the USS JOHN F. KENNEDY, CV-67, and both carried CVW-3's AC tail code. VA-46, known as the Clansmen, flew aircraft with modex numbers in the 3XX series, while the Blue Hawks of VA-72 used modex numbers in the 4XX series. In closing out the Corsair

*An A-7E receives fuel from an Air Force tanker during a mission over Kuwait. Cooperation between the Air Force, Navy, Marines, and coalition air forces was excellent throughout the campaign. Note the two Sidewinder missiles on their launch rails. (DOD)*

II's service with the Navy, VA-46 flew 355 combat missions, and VA-72 flew 362 for a total of 717. None of the twenty-four Corsairs assigned to these two squadrons were lost to enemy action or to non-combat related causes.

The two A-7 squadrons expended over two million pounds of ordnance against Iraqi targets, to include airfields, Scud production and storage areas, munitions stockpiles, power plants, troop concentrations, nuclear research facilities, railroad yards, and supply lines. They also flew SAM suppression missions using AGM-88 HARM missiles.

AIM-9L/-M Sidewinders were usually carried for self defense on the two fuselage stations. When carried, 300-gallon external fuel tanks were normally attached to the inboard wing pylons, but in some cases, only one of these tanks was carried. It was usually attached to the left inboard station. Often, when pylons were not used to carry stores, they were removed from the aircraft.

Although they did not deliver any laser guided bombs, the A-7Es did employ the electro-optically guided AGM-62 Walleye II. Photographs show only one of these missiles being carried on each aircraft, and it was mounted on the left center pylon. The right center pylon was empty, and all other wing pylons were removed. Up to four AGM-88 HARMs were carried on the outer and center wing stations.

Triple Ejector Racks, (TER), were often attached to the outboard pylons. Three Mk 82, 500-pound bombs or three Mk 20 Rockeyes were usually carried on each of these racks, and sometimes additional Mk 82s or Mk 20s would be loaded singly on the center and/or inboard wing pylons. Up to four Mk 83, 1000-pound bombs or four Mk 84, 2000-pound bombs were carried singly on the center and outboard wing pylons. On some missions, two ADM-141 TALD decoys were carried as part of the weapons load to fool enemy defenses.

A-7Es from VA-72 and a single A-6E from VA-75 refuel from an Air Force KC-135 enroute to their targets. The A-6E will escort the A-7Es and will serve as a tanker later in the mission if needed. All but one of the A-7Es are armed with four Mk 83, 1000-pound bombs and two Sidewinder missiles. One A-7E, number 407, is carrying four HARM anti-radiation missiles to suppress enemy air defenses if needed. The squadron's CAG aircraft is also in the photograph, and it is distinguished by the checkerboard markings on its rudder.

(Official U.S. Navy photograph by CDR John "Lites" Leenhouts)

Two of the scoreboards on the A-7Es seen in the photograph above are illustrated in these close-ups. At left is number 407, which is the aircraft carrying the HARM missiles in the top photo. At right is number 410, which is the aircraft in the background behind the A-6E.

(Both are Official U.S. Navy photographs by PH3 Paul A. Hawthorne)

# AV-8B HARRIER

*The Marines operated AV-8B Harriers from land bases and from the USS NASSAU, LHA-4, during Operation Desert Storm. This AV-8B was photographed on the flight deck of the NASSAU between missions.*　　　*(DOD)*

Five squadrons of USMC AV-8B Harriers participated in Operation Desert Storm. VMA-231, VMA-311, VMA-531 (Detachment B), and VMA-542 were ground based at King Abdul Aziz Naval Base and had forward operating locations at Tanajib and Kabrit, Saudi Arabia. VMA-331 became the first USMC Harrier squadron ever to operate from a ship during combat when they flew missions from the USS NASSAU, LHA-4. These five squadrons began the war with eighty-eight aircraft and flew 3,383 missions. They delivered almost six million pounds of ordnance against Iraqi targets.

AV-8Bs suffered the highest number of losses of any U.S. aircraft type during the war. Six were lost in combat, while two more were destroyed in non-combat related crashes. The com-

bat losses were due to the fact that the Harrier's engine exhausts are near the center of the aircraft. A shoulder-fired surface-to-air missile with infrared guidance would usually hit the Harrier near these exhausts, and this would cause damage to vital components of the aircraft. All AV-8B combat losses came as a result of hits by these small shoulder-fired missiles. By comparison, aircraft with their engine exhausts in the tail section had a much higher survivability rate, because hits by the same types of missiles often did not damage vital parts of the aircraft and therefore did not cause lethal damage.

Although launch rails were usually fitted to both outboard wing pylons, Harriers carried only one AIM-9L or -M on the left pylon. The fuselage-mounted 25-mm gun system appears to have been installed most of the time, although some photos of AV-8Bs taken in Saudi Arabia show them without it.

The middle and inboard wing pylons were usually used to carry Mk 82 and Mk 83 standard bombs as well as Rockeye cluster bombs. To ignite oil in Iraqi defensive trenches, Mk 77 napalm was used. CBU-55 or CBU-72 Fuel Air Explosive (FAE) bombs were employed to detonate Iraqi mine fields.

One report also indicated that a few (less than ten) AGM-65E Maverick missiles were fired from Harriers. Unlike other versions of the Maverick, the AGM-65E is used only by the Marines and is painted gray. It is guided to its target by a ground-based laser designator that is operated by troops that are being supported by the Harrier. Other reports state that GBU-12D and GBU-16B laser guided bombs were dropped from Harriers, and that both 2.75 and 5-inch rocket pods were also used. However, these also appear to have been used in very limited numbers.

*Five Harriers fly in formation behind an Air Force tanker before moving in to take on fuel.*　　　*(USAF)*

*Coverage of the AV-8B Harrier continues on page 41.*

# COLOR GALLERY

Two F-117As are parked on the ramp at their air base at Khamis Mushait, Saudi Arabia. The aircraft in the background is assigned to the wing commander, and is also the subject of the photographs below. The F-117A in the foreground is painted in more standard markings for the 37th TFW.

*(USAF)*

The wing commander's aircraft is shown at left as it returned to Nellis AFB, Nevada, shortly after the war ended. The photograph at right illustrates the art work on the inside of the left bomb bay door and shows that the aircraft was named *THE TOXIC AVENGER.* A close-up of the mission markings on this aircraft can be found on the rear cover.

*(Both Isham)*

A Nighthawk is towed from its shelter prior to a mission. Note the open bomb bay doors and the extended "trapeze" or bomb rack.

*(USAF)*

An F-14A+ Tomcat from VF-74 and Carrier Air Wing Seventeen is fully armed and ready for a mission from USS SARATOGA. Note the colors and markings of the AIM-54 Phoenix air-to-air missile under the fuselage. An AIM-9 Sidewinder and an AIM-7 Sparrow can be seen on the wing glove pylon. (DOD)

An A-6E Intruder from VA-35 carries mission markings on its fuselage just aft of the cockpit to indicate its participation in Operation Desert Storm. A close-up of these markings can be found on the rear cover. VA-35 was assigned to Carrier Air Wing Seventeen and the USS SARATOGA during Operations Desert Shield and Desert Storm. (Flightleader)

More aircraft from Carrier Air Wing Seventeen can be seen on SARATOGA's flight deck in this view. In the foreground is the CAG F/A-18 from VFA-83, while beyond it is another of that squadron's Hornets. A KA-6D tanker, an SH-3H Sea King helicopter, and an A-6E Intruder are also visible in the background. The KA-6D and A-6E belong to VA-35, while the SH-3H is assigned to HS-3. (DOD)

An A-6E TRAM prepares to launch from the USS THEODORE ROOSEVELT during the ship's deployment in support of Operations Desert Storm and Provide Comfort. Fitted with four external fuel tanks and a buddy refueling store on the centerline, this aircraft will fly a support mission to provide fuel to other aircraft. A-6Es were often used as tankers during Desert Storm.

*(Official U.S. Navy photograph by PHC Denis Keske)*

Although the A-7E Corsair II illustrated in the front cover photograph has been well documented, the squadron commander's aircraft for VA-46 was also painted in special markings as the USS JOHN F. KENNEDY returned from Desert Storm. A-7E, 160714, was painted in the gloss gull gray over white paint scheme used on Navy Corsair IIs when they first entered service. It became the last A-7 to be painted in colorful markings which were also reminiscent of the Corsair's early service. These two photographs show this A-7E on the KENNEDY's flight deck as the ship headed back home. Note the mission markings on the nose of the aircraft.

*(Official U.S. Navy Photographs by PH3 Paul A. Hawthorne)*

*Above: F-15C, 85-102, was one of four aircraft named GULF SPIRIT, and it served as the wing commander's aircraft for the 33rd Tactical Fighter Wing. It is shown here after it returned to the unit's home at Eglin Air Force Base, Florida. It is configured with AIM-120A AMRAAM missiles on its wing pylons in place of Sidewinders.* (Detail & Scale collection)

*Right: This close-up shows the kill markings and nose art on the F-15 shown above. The green star next to COL Rick Parsons' name is for the victory COL Parsons scored. The small white lettering in the star reads 7 FEB 91 Su-22. COL Parsons was flying another aircraft, F-15C, 85-124, when he scored the kill. The three Iraqi flags represent the three kills scored in this particular aircraft, F-15C, 85-102. The one on the left is for a MiG-23 that was shot down by CPT David G. Rose using an AIM-7 Sparrow on January 29, 1991. The other two flags are for two Su-22s shot down by CPT Anthony R. Murphy on February 7, 1991. AIM-7s were also used for these two kills.* (Lore)

*Above: Perhaps the most active F-15E Strike Eagle during Operation Desert Storm was 87-0209. It flew at least 55 combat missions as indicated by the bomb markings painted on its fuselage just below the canopy. This photograph was taken just after the aircraft returned to Seymour Johnson Air Force Base after the war.*

*Right: This close-up shows the mission markings on the side of 87-0209. Each bomb indicates five combat missions.*

The General Dynamics F-111F was far and away the most successful aircraft during the war. Sixty-six of these aircraft from the 48th Tactical Fighter Wing destroyed more targets than any other type of aircraft. This is the wing commander's aircraft over the Saudi desert. A close-up of the mission markings on this aircraft appears on the rear cover of this book. *(USAF)*

 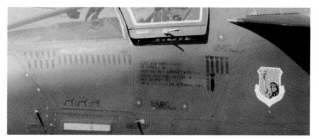

At left is F-111F, 73-710, as it appeared in mid-February 1991 at Taif Air Base, Saudi Arabia. It is being loaded with GBU-12 laser guided bombs. At right is a close-up of the mission markings on this aircraft. Different types of bombs are painted in black under the windshield and just aft of the aircraft data block. The destruction of three hardened aircraft shelters is symbolized just above the formation light panel. The shelters are painted black and have a bomb entering the roof. A red flame or explosion is painted around the shelter. *(Both Drummond)*

Above: EF-111A, 66-030, still had its combat markings when it returned to Mountain Home Air Force Base after the war. Forty mission symbols are painted under the canopy. These were removed shortly after the aircraft arrived back in the United States. *(Drummond)*

Right: This photograph illustrates the style of mission markings used on EF-111As of the 390th ECS. Only one 42nd ECS Raven carried mission or other combat markings, and that was 66-056. *(Drummond)*

With its refueling receptacle open, an A-10A moves in to refuel from a tanker before heading on to its target. An ALQ-119 ECM pod can be seen on station 11, while Maverick missiles are attached to stations 3 and 9. Two Sidewinder air-to-air missiles are on station 1. *(USAF)*

*This Warthog belongs to the 706th TFS, 926th TFG. A close-up of the nose art on this aircraft appears on the rear cover.* *(Bell)*

*During Desert Storm, the B-52G dropped more bombs than any other type of aircraft. This Stratofortress is from the 416th Bomb Wing at Griffis AFB, New York. A close-up of the Desert Storm nose art and mission markings for this aircraft can be found on the rear cover.*
*(Flightleader)*

*The New York Air National Guard's 138th TFS was one of several Guard units that participated in the war effort, and one of their F-16As is shown here after it returned to the United States. Note the ALQ-119 ECM pod under the left wing of this aircraft. A close-up of the mission markings that were painted on the nose gear door of this aircraft appears on the rear cover.* (Flightleader)

*One of the RF-4Cs from the 117th Tactical Reconnaissance Wing that saw plenty of flight time during Desert Shield and Desert Storm was 65-833 shown here. It had a red, white, and black shark's mouth and eyes on the nose, while most other aircraft from this unit carried shark's mouths and eyes that were in subdued shades of gray. A close-up of the mission markings that were painted on the aircraft's left intake ramp can be found on the rear cover.*

*Mission markings were painted on the left inlet ramp of this F-4G Wild Weasel from the 52nd TFW. It is shown here on public display after the war, and has HARM missiles on its inboard wing pylons.*
*(Detail & Scale collection)*

Aircraft were not the only things adorned with special art during Desert Storm. Carrying on a tradition that dates almost as far back as the military use of aircraft, ground and air crews painted faces and messages on the ordnance carried by the aircraft. This art work varied from the simple to the elaborate. At left is a Mk 84, 2000-pound bomb with a shark's mouth and eyes drawn on it. It is quite simple, and it appears that either chalk or a grease pencil was used. At right is a fancier rendition of the same type of thing. The art work was only on one side of the bomb. *(Both USAF)*

A couple of artists displayed their work on this Mk 84. One used a white piece of chalk or grease pencil to reassure any Iraqi soldiers that the bomb would not cause them any pain, while another tried to provide some therapy to help the Iraqis have a better outlook on life. *(USAF)*

PUCKER UP **and a pair of lips were painted on this 2000-pound bomb.** *(USAF)*

Personal messages to Saddam Hussein were often seen on the ordnance. White spray paint was used on these CBU-89A/Bs to send messages to the Iraqi leader. A black marker was also used to write a smaller but more adamant message on the upper cluster bomb unit. *(USAF)*

More messages to Saddam Hussein and the Iraqis in general are written on this GBU-24A. The photograph also shows the colors of the bomb and its guidance section to good effect.

*(Detail & Scale collection)*

*This AV-8B prepares to take off from the flight deck of the NASSAU for a mission during Operation Desert Shield.*

*(Official U.S. Navy Photograph)*

*These four Harriers are lined up for take off from the NASSAU, and the lack of ordnance would indicate that this was a training mission flown during Desert Shield.*

*(DOD)*

*The black bomb silhouette on the side of this Harrier has a white 39 painted on it to indicate the number of combat missions the aircraft has flown. This photograph was taken when the aircraft made a visit to the USS JOHN F. KENNEDY during Desert Storm.*

*(Official U.S. Navy photograph by PH3 Paul A. Hawthorne)*

# A-10 WARTHOG

*Carrying everything from AIM-9 Sidewinder missiles to cluster bombs, and ECM pods to Maverick missiles, the A-10 Warthog undoubtedly carried the widest variety of external stores during Operation Desert Storm. At left, an A-10 prowls the skies above the desert armed with a single AIM-9, two cluster bombs, and two Mavericks. An ALQ-119 is on the right outboard station. At right, armorers prepare to load the A-10's huge GAU-8, 30-mm gun, while other crewmen attach a Rockeye cluster bomb under the wing.*

*(Both USAF)*

The A-10 Warthog is generally considered to have very little eye appeal, and it has long been the brunt of many jokes. It is slow—so slow that it is said to be the only Air Force aircraft to take bird strikes from the rear! But by all measures, the A-10 and the OA-10 performed admirably during Operation Desert Storm. While they may appear to be ugly to others, they must have been beautiful to the pilots who flew them back from combat with damage that would have brought down just about any other aircraft.

Seven squadrons of Warthogs participated in Operation Desert Storm. Six of these flew the standard A-10, while the seventh (the 23rd TASS of the 602nd TACW) operated the externally identical OA-10. The table at the bottom of this page summarizes the units that flew the Warthogs during the Gulf War.

During Desert Storm these units operated from King Fahd Airport in northeast Saudi Arabia, and were assigned to the 354th Tactical Fighter Wing (Provisional). They operated 144 Warthogs, of which five were lost in combat. There were no non-combat losses of A-10s or OA-10s. Over 8,500 sorties were flown by these aircraft, and they delivered no less than 23,927 bombs and cluster bombs as well as 5,013 AGM-65 Maverick missiles.

A-10s proved their versatility during the war as they performed a wide variety of missions. Most missions were flown to destroy tanks and other vehicles. Artillery pieces, anti-aircraft guns, and surface-to-air missile sites also came under attacks by the Warthogs. A-10s also hunted for Scuds and accounted for the only two aerial victories scored by a gun system during the war. In both of these cases the victims were Iraqi helicopters. Once the ground war began, A-10s flew close air support missions for the ground troops.

Because the A-10 has eleven weapons stations, it can carry a wide variety of stores in combinations that are seemingly endless. It is not possible to cover all of these in such a limited space, but the following information should prove helpful. It should be noted that the stations are numbered one through eleven, beginning with the left outboard wing station.

Station one usually carried two AIM-9L or -M Sidewinders mounted on a dual rail adapter. As the war continued and the Iraqi air threat was not considered great, this was often reduced to a single missile on the outer rail. Station eleven carried an ALQ-119 long ECM pod. One report has indicated that European based units carried the ALQ-131 shallow ECM pod instead, but photos show these aircraft with the ALQ-119. A few photographs

*An A-10 pilot follows the directions of a member of the ramp crew as he taxis back to his position after a mission over Kuwait. Although ALQ-119 ECM pods were usually carried under the right wing on station 11, they were occasionally attached to station 1 under the left wing as seen here.*

*(USAF)*

*At left is an overall view of one of the OA-10s flown by the 602nd TACW from Davis-Monthan AFB, Arizona. At right is a close-up of the nose art on the aircraft. It consists of the name Angel and a stylized Arizona state flag.*

*(Both Bell)*

have shown this arrangement reversed with the Sidewinders on station eleven and the ALQ-119 on station one.

Stations two and ten were seldom used, and were often seen removed from the aircraft to improve maneuverability. Stations three and nine were used to carry Mavericks, and these were most often loaded singly on LAU-117 launch rails. However, triple-rail LAU-88s were also used on these stations, but only two Mavericks were attached to each. These were slant loaded with one missile on the lower rail and one on the outboard rail. Mavericks were usually mixed half and half between EO and IIR versions.

When used, triple ejector racks (TER) were carried only on stations four and eight. While these racks can carry three bombs, they were normally seen with two. Much of the time these were flat loaded with the bombs on the shoulder positions of the TERs,

but in other cases they were slant loaded with the bombs on the lower and outboard positions. Stations five and seven were used only to carry single bombs or cluster bomb units, and were sometimes removed from the aircraft. Station six was not used in combat.

Single bombs and cluster bombs were often carried on stations three, four, five, seven, eight, and nine. Only one type of these weapons was carried per mission, however, they were sometimes mixed with Maverick missiles. The most common types of standard ordance carried included Mk 82 LDGP bombs, Mk 20 Rockeyes, and SUU-30H cluster bomb dispensers. Except for stations one and eleven as noted above, the ordnance loads were balanced. That is to say, whatever was on station three was also on station nine. What was carried on station four was also loaded on station eight, and stations five and seven would also be the same.

## A-10 SQUADRONS IN OPERATION DESERT STORM

| SQUADRON | WING | TAIL CODE | HOME BASE |
| --- | --- | --- | --- |
| 23rd TASS | 602nd TACW | NF | Davis Monthan AFB, AZ |
| 74th TFS | 23rd TFW | EL | England AFB, LA |
| 76th TFS | 23rd TFW | EL | England AFB, LA |
| 353rd TFS | 354th TFW | MB | Myrtle Beach, SC |
| 355th TFS | 354th TFW | MB | Myrtle Beach, SC |
| 511th TFS | 10th TFW | AR | RAF Alconbury, UK |
| 706th TFS | 926th TFG | NO | NAS New Orleans, LA |

*The wing commander's aircraft from the 23rd TFW sustained considerable damage to its tail section as shown in these two views. However, it returned safely to its base.*

*(Both USAF)*

# B-52G STRATOFORTRESS

*The heavy bomber used by the U.S. Air Force during Desert Storm was the B-52G. The B-52H, which has better nuclear delivery capabilities, remained on nuclear alert with the B-1B during the war. The contention put forth by B-1 critics and the news media that the B-1B should have been used in Operation Desert Storm was ridiculous. It would have been unwise to take America's only true penetrator bomber off nuclear alert and send it to the Middle East when the B-52G was more than capable of doing the job.* (USAF)

As was the case in the previous limited wars in Korea and Vietnam, a big strategic bomber was needed to deliver large bomb loads during Operation Desert Storm. In early 1991, when Operation Desert Storm took place, the Soviet Union was still in tact, and the Strategic Air Command was tasked with keeping bombers on nuclear alert. With the last of its FB-111As being transferred to the Tactical Air Command, SAC had B-1B Lancers, B-52Hs, and B-52Gs in its inventory. There were only ninety-seven B-1Bs available, and as SAC's only truly capable penetrators, they had to remain on nuclear alert and in their training roles for that mission. Further, the conventional weapons delivery capability of the Lancer had not become operational at that time, but even if it had, the B-1Bs would have had to remain on nuclear alert.

Of the two remaining variants of the B-52 Stratofortress that remained in the inventory, the B-52H had the greater capability to carry out nuclear delivery missions against the Soviets, and this was considered its primary role. The delivery of conventional weapons was secondary. However, the B-52Gs had been assigned to support conventional operations, therefore, it was the B-52G that was selected for use in the Gulf War.

The mission performed by the B-52G that received the most coverage in the media was that of carpet bombing the Iraqi Republican Guards, but the Stratofortresses also hit airfields, industrial complexes, storage areas, oil refineries, rail yards, and other area targets. They flew 1,624 missions and dropped 25,700 tons of bombs. This represented almost thirty percent of the total tonnage delivered during the war.

The following units flew B-52Gs during Desert Storm:

| BOMB WING | BOMB SQUADRON | HOME BASE |
| --- | --- | --- |
| 2nd BW | 62nd BS | Barksdale AFB, LA |
| 2nd BW | 596th BS | Barksdale AFB, LA |
| 42nd BW | 69th BS | Loring AFB, ME |
| 93rd BW | 328th BS | Castle AFB, CA |
| 97th BW | 340th BS | Eaker AFB, AR |
| 379th BW | 524th BS | Wurtsmith AFB, MI |
| 416th BW | 688th BS | Griffiss AFB, NY |

The units operated from several bases as they flew missions against targets in Iraq and Kuwait. The 2nd, 93rd, 379th, and 416th Bomb Wings flew out of RAF Fairford, United Kingdom. The 379th and 416th Bomb Wings also operated from Moron Air Base, Spain, as well. The 42nd and 97th Bomb Wings flew from Diego Garcia. All units except the 97th Bomb Wing flew missions from King Abdul Aziz Airport at Jeddah in southwestern Saudi Arabia. There are also reports that a few missions were flown from Cairo West Air Base in Egypt. Only one B-52G was lost in over 1,600 missions, and that was not due to combat.

Up to fifty-one bombs could be carried on a single B-52G, with twenty-four carried externally on two pylons and twenty-seven carried in the bomb bay. This was significantly less than the "big belly" B-52Ds carried in Vietnam, but it was far larger than any other aircraft that operated during Desert Storm. A summary of bombs and cluster bombs dropped by the B-52G is

*At left, a cell of three B-52Gs taxis out to the active runway for a mission to bomb Iraqi targets. At right, a B-52G takes off on a mission.*
*(USAF)*

A B-52G tops off its fuel tanks on its way home after a mission. (USAF)

included in the following table. The number indicates the actual bomb count rather than tons or pounds.

| TYPE OF BOMB | NUMBER DELIVERED |
|---|---|
| M117 750-pound bomb | 44,660 |
| Mk 82 500-pound bomb | 17,678 |
| CBU-52 cluster bomb | 2,939 |
| CBU-58 cluster bomb | 5,931 |
| CBU-71/-87/-89 cluster bombs | 804 |
| British 1000-pound bomb | 287 |
| Total | 72,299 |

Because of the length of the weapons, the load was reduced to thirty-six when CBU-87s or CBU-89s were carried. A reduced load was also necessary when aircraft based at Diego Garcia dropped eight loads of British 1000-pound bombs.

It was proposed that B-52Gs be armed with GBU-12s that would be guided against Iraqi tanks by F-111Fs or F-15Es. However, the war ended before this could be put into effect.

One year after the war began, the Air Force announced that seven B-52Gs of the 2nd Bomb Wing based at Barksdale AFB, Louisiana, had flown the longest combat missions in history. The B-52Gs took off at 6:35 a.m. Central Time, thus becoming the first aircraft to be launched in support of Operation Desert Storm. They flew a total distance of more than 14,000 miles and remained aloft for more than thirty-five hours. Four in-flight refuelings were required--two in each direction. From positions about fifty miles south of the Iraqi-Saudi border, and well outside the Iraqi defense network, these Stratofortresses launched thirty-five conventionally armed AGM-86C Air Launched Cruise Missiles (ALCM) at high-priority targets in Iraq. It is reported that at least thirty of these hit their targets.

The AGM-86C version of the ALCM became operational in 1988 and was developed by modifying existing nuclear cruise missiles to carry a 1000-pound, high-explosive, blast-fragmentation warhead. This was the first combat use of the ALCM, and they supplemented the fifty-one sea-launched Tomahawk cruise missiles that were fired in the opening attacks that first night. Targets included power generating and transmission facilities as well as military communications sites near Mosul, in northern Iraq. All ALCMs were carried internally, and this was reportedly for security reasons.

*On the opening night of the war, seven B-52Gs from Barksdale Air Force Base, Louisiana, flew over 14,000 miles to launch AGM-86C Air Launched Cruise Missiles (ALCM) at high priority targets in Iraq.* (USAF)

# ARMAMENT

## LASER GUIDED BOMBS

The photograph at left shows GBU-10Cs attached to the wing pylons of an F-111F. The GBU-10E and -F have the same external appearance. GBU-10s are of the 2000 class, and the -C, -E, and -F versions are based on the standard Mk 84 like the earlier GBU-10A and -B. GBU-10G, -H, and -Js are based on the more cylindrical BLU-109 warhead but use the same guidance and wing sections as the GBU-10C, -E, and -F. The GBU-10B and subsequent variants (known as Paveway IIs) were the versions used during Operation Desert Storm. They were overall olive drab with a standard three-inch yellow nose band next to the nose adapter. The one exception to this was that the GBU-10J had its band located at the front of the cylindrical section of its BLU-109 warhead where the taper began rather than next to the nose adapter. Identification stripes, which were actually one-inch by three-inch rectangles, were painted on both sides of the nose adapter, the left side of the canards, and the top left wing glove. A close-up of the wing section is shown at right, and the small identification stripe can be seen painted on the upper left wing glove.          (Left Detail & Scale collection, right author)

### GBU-10C, -D, -E, & -F (wings deployed)
### Mk 84 warhead

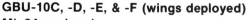

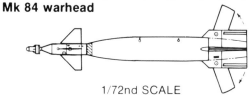

1/72nd SCALE

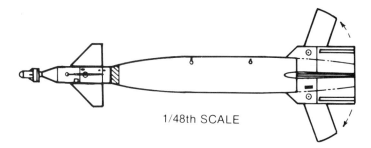

1/48th SCALE

### GBU-10G, -H, & -J (wings stowed)
### BLU-109 warhead

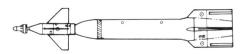

1/72nd SCALE

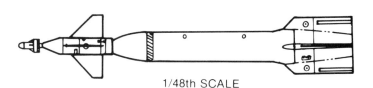

1/48th SCALE

GBU-12s are based on the Mk 82, 500-pound bomb, and it was the externally identical GBU-12B, -C, and -D variants that were used in Operation Desert Storm. Two of these weapons are shown here on an F-111F at Tiaf Air Base, Saudi Arabia. GBU-12B, -C, and -Ds were olive drab with standard three-inch yellow nose bands. The ID stripes or rectangles were one inch by three inches, and were painted orange.          (Drummond)

This photograph shows a GBU-12 on a display stand with its wings extended.          (USAF)

### GBU-12B, -C, & -D (wings deployed)
### Mk 82 warhead

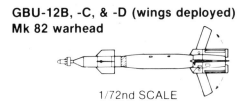

1/72nd SCALE

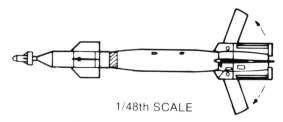

1/48th SCALE

The GBU-16 is a combination of the Navy's Mk 83, 1000-pound bomb and the GBU-10C guidance and wing sections. It is used only by Navy and Marine aircraft and is shown here under the wing of an A-6E Intruder. It is painted the same as the GBU-10 and GBU-12 guided bombs.

## GBU-16A, & -B (wings deployed)
## Mk 83 warhead

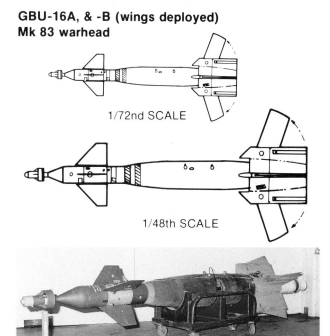

1/72nd SCALE

1/48th SCALE

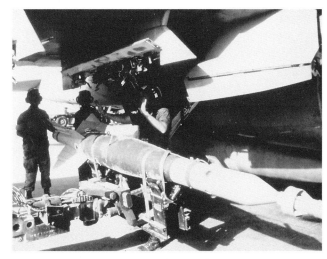

The AGM-123A Skipper is an adaptation of the GBU-16 shown above. A small rocket motor is attached to the wing section to give the weapon more standoff range than is attainable with unpowered guided bombs, and its AGM designation would indicate its classification in the air-to-ground missile category. Skippers seen during the war had an olive drab warhead and a gray (FS 36375) guidance and motor section as shown in this view. Although this photograph has been published before, it has been misidentified as a GBU-16 instead of an AGM-123. The photograph shows a Skipper being loaded on an A-6E Intruder during the war. (USAF)

A better look at the AGM-123A is provided by this photograph of a Skipper on a cart at the Naval Weapons Center at China Lake, California. (Official U.S. Navy Photograph)

## AGM-123A SKIPPER II (wings deployed)
## Mk 83 warhead

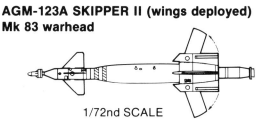

1/72nd SCALE

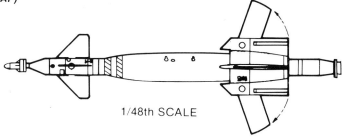

1/48th SCALE

## GBU-24 (wings deployed)
## Mk 84 warhead

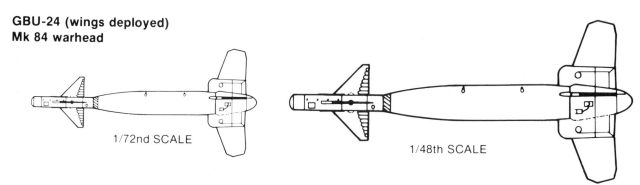

1/72nd SCALE

1/48th SCALE

Like the GBU-10 series of laser guided bombs, the GBU-24s also are in the 2000-pound class and use both the Mk 84 and BLU-109 warheads. These photographs illustrate the GBU-24 which utilizes the Mk 84 standard bomb as its warhead. The photograph at right was taken from behind to show the offset wing arrangement used on the GBU-24 weapons.                    (Detail & Scale collection)

## GBU-24A (wings stowed)
## BLU-109 warhead (rotated 45 degrees)

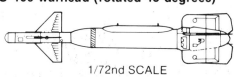

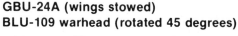

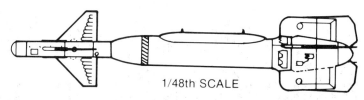

1/72nd SCALE

1/48th SCALE

The GBU-24A uses the BLU-109 warhead and the same guidance and wing sections of the Mk 84 GBU-24. However, because of its thinner body, an adapter, often called the hardback, must be fitted on the warhead to provide adequate clearance between the wing section and the pylon. Another difference is on the wing section where it mates with the aft end of the BLU-109. An extended "sawtooth" area is added to insure a proper fit. This is not needed on the Mk 84 GBU-24, because the Mk 84 bomb body is more tapered at its aft end. GBU-24s of both types used during the Gulf War were painted olive drab and had ID stripes (rectangles) and nose bands in the locations as previously described for the GBU-10s. As the photographs illustrate, the nose band was further back on the version using the BLU-109 penetrator warhead.

(Left Detail & Scale collection, right Drummond)

**GBU-27 (wings deployed)**
**Mk 84 warhead**

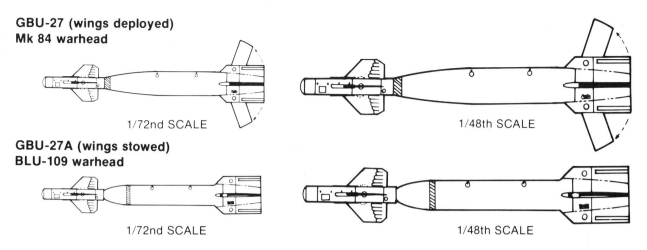

1/72nd SCALE

1/48th SCALE

**GBU-27A (wings stowed)**
**BLU-109 warhead**

1/72nd SCALE

1/48th SCALE

*The GBU-27 laser guided bombs are derivatives of the GBU-24 which are intended for use with the F-117A. Again, the 2000-pound Mk 84 and BLU-109 are used as warheads for these weapons. The guidance section is attached to the warhead using an adapter ring that is 6.75 inches long instead of the nine inches used on the GBU-24. Also, the canards are clipped at the trailing tip, and it appears that their span is a little less than that used on the GBU-24. The wing section for the GBU-27s is the same as used on the GBU-10, and this eliminates the need for the GBU-24A's hardback and sawtooth extension.*

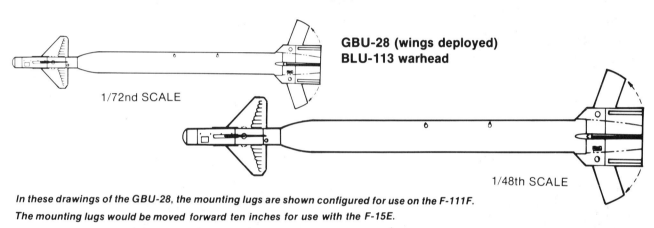

**GBU-28 (wings deployed)**
**BLU-113 warhead**

1/72nd SCALE

1/48th SCALE

*In these drawings of the GBU-28, the mounting lugs are shown configured for use on the F-111F.*
*The mounting lugs would be moved forward ten inches for use with the F-15E.*

*The GBU-28 "Deep Throat" bombs were developed during the war at a record pace. They consisted of an Army howitzer barrel that had been sized to accept the same wing unit used on the GBU-10 and GBU-27. A nose section was added, and an adapter collar was attached to accept the same guidance unit used on the GBU-27. The bore was enlarged to accept 675 pounds of tritonal explosive. The resulting weapon offered a precision guided bomb that could penetrate bunkers buried over 100 feet under ground. Only two were used in combat during the war, and they are shown in these two photographs. At left is an overall view of the bombs before the guidance sections were attached. At right is the stencilled data on the side of one of the bombs. Note that the total weight of the weapon is 4,485 pounds, and that it carries 675 pounds of explosives. The warhead is shown as a BLU-109 SPECIAL, but it has since been redesignated BLU-113. The bombs were delivered by two F-111Fs of the 48th TFW.*                    *(Both Detail & Scale collection)*

# ELECTRO-OPTICALLY GUIDED BOMBS

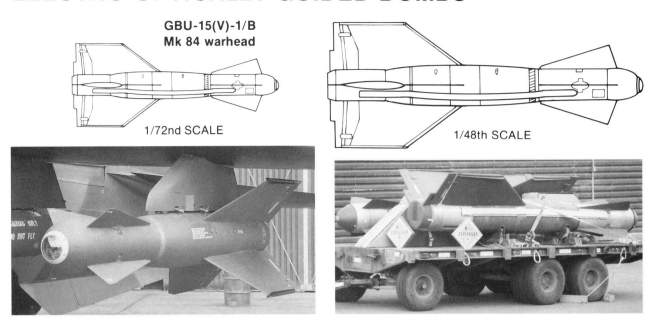

GBU-15(V)-1/B
Mk 84 warhead

1/72nd SCALE

1/48th SCALE

*Electro-optically guided bombs carry a television camera in their nose section. This camera sends back images to the pilot or weapon systems operator who has a "weapon's eye view" of the target from the camera. The link between the aircraft and the weapon is provided by an AXQ-14 Data Link Pod which is carried externally on the aircraft. The most publicized use of electro-optically guided weapons during Operation Desert Storm was when GBU-15s were dropped by F-111Fs to destroy the manifolds which were dumping oil into the Arabian Gulf. At left is a GBU-15(V)-2 under the left wing of an F-111F. This version of the GBU-15 uses the Mk 84, 2000-pound bomb for its warhead. The "eye" for the camera is clearly visible on the nose. At right, two GBU-15s wait to be loaded on an aircraft. Note the protective covers over the camera lens. GBU-15s were overall olive drab as were the AXQ-14s. Some, but not all, have a 3-inch yellow band on the warhead just behind the guidance section.*     *(Left Detail & Scale collection, right USAF)*

## AGM-62 WALLEYE I ER/DL

## AGM-62 WALLEYE II ER/DL

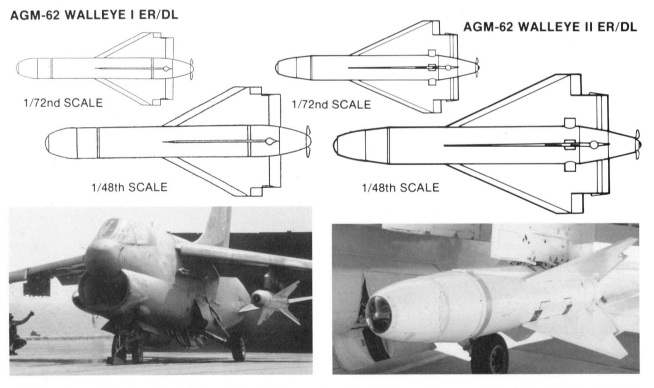

1/72nd SCALE

1/72nd SCALE

1/48th SCALE

1/48th SCALE

*The other electro-optically guided bomb used in the Gulf War was the AGM-62 Walleye. Evidence indicates that both Walleye I ER/DLs and Walleye II ER/DLs were used, but not the standard Walleye I or Walleye II. Walleyes were guided by the AWW-9 Data Link Pod. The weapons were usually overall gloss white, but the nose sections and wings were sometimes light gray. The AWW-9 data link pods were white with light gray forward and rear radomes. At left is a photograph of an A-7E Corsair II being readied for launch from the USS JOHN F. KENNEDY during Operation Desert Storm. The aircraft is from VA-72, and it carries a Walleye I ER/DL under its left wing. The data link pod was often carried by a second aircraft that would stand off a safe distance from the target area. At right is a close-up of a Walleye II ER/DL.*     *(Official U.S. Navy Photographs)*

# STANDARD BOMBS

**Mk 82 LDGP (M904 fuse)**
**(fins rotated 45 degrees)**

1/72nd SCALE          1/48th SCALE

**Mk 82 SNAKEYE (M904 fuse)**
**(fins rotated 45 degrees)**

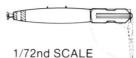 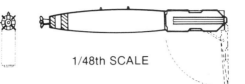 

1/72nd SCALE          1/48th SCALE

*The 500-pound class of Mk 82 general purpose bombs is used by the Air Force, Navy, and Marines with a variety of fuses and tail sections. At left is a low-drag general purpose (LDGP) bomb on an F/A-18 Hornet. Note the rough exterior on this bomb which is common to most bombs now in the Navy's inventory. This rough exterior is a thermal protective covering to help prevent the bomb from "cooking off" in the event of a fire. The Navy started adding this coating after fires aboard the carriers FORRESTAL and ENTERPRISE detonated bombs on the flight deck causing extensive damage to the ships. Navy bombs with this coating also have two, three-inch nose bands instead of the usual single band. The FS 36375 gray low-drag tail section was common on Navy and Marine bombs used in Desert Storm. At right is another Mk 82 with the original high drag tail section. These high-drag bombs were called Snakeyes. They are no longer used by the Air Force, but remain in the inventories of the Navy and Marines.*

*(Left Official U.S. Navy Photograph, right author)*

**Mk 82 AIR (nose plug)**
**(fins rotated 45 degrees)**

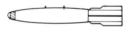  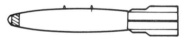

1/72nd SCALE

1/48th SCALE

*The Air Force has replaced the Snakeyes with Mk 82 AIR or Air Inflatable Retard bombs. These weapons have a larger diameter tail section which contains a small parachute. This parachute deploys when the bomb is dropped and retards the bomb's forward flight more effectively and dependably than the Snakeye's clamshell type fins. Here an F-111F drops Mk 82 AIR bombs on the practice range.      (USAF)*

*These two photographs show the details of the Mk 82 AIR to good effect. Note the smooth shell of the Air Force bomb in the photograph at left. The AIR tail section is illustrated in the photograph at right. These two photographs were taken of bombs loaded on an F-111F. They are attached to a BRU or Bomb Release Unit.*

*(Both Detail & Scale collection)*

**M117R (MAU-91 fin)**

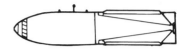

1/72nd SCALE                    1/48th SCALE

*M117, 750-pound bombs are used only by the Air Force, and during Operation Desert Storm, they were delivered in large numbers by B-52Gs. Indications are that two different tail sections were used. The MAU-91A/B or B/B tail assembly is a selectable low drag or high drag device that has four extendable metal drag plates. This configuration provides the pilot or bombardier with a selectable high drag or low drag option through the Nose/Tail Arm switch. If the low drag option is selected, the drag plates are held in place by a retaining band and remain closed during delivery. If the crew selects the high drag option, the release band latch is pulled by a lanyard attached to the arming solenoid, and the plates spring open when the bomb is released in much the same manner as those on the Mk 82 Snakeye.*          *(USAF)*

**M117 (MAU-103 fin)**
**(fins rotated 45 degrees)**

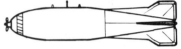

1/72nd SCALE                    1/48th SCALE

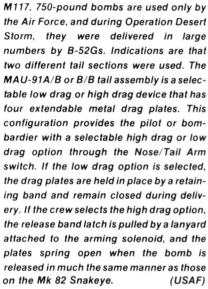

*A low drag general purpose fin section used during the Gulf War was the MAU-103A/B, and it is seen on these M117s. This is different from the low drag tail sections used on the same type of bombs during the war in Vietnam.*

*(USS KENNEDY Photo Lab)*

**Mk 83 LDGP (M904 fuse)**
**(fins rotated 45 degrees)**

1/72nd SCALE

1/48th SCALE

*The Mk 83, 1000-pound bombs are used exclusively by the Navy and Marines. The only tail section used with these bombs is the low drag type shown here. While the rough flame retardant surface is difficult to see in this photograph, the two nose bands indicate that these bombs do have the protective coating. Beginning in the 1980s, the tail sections of many Navy/Marine bombs were painted FS 36375 gray as seen here.*
*(USAF)*

**Mk 84 LDGP (M904 fuse)**
**(fins rotated 45 degrees)**

1/72nd SCALE

1/48th SCALE

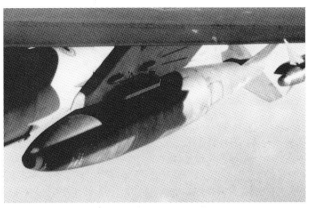

The Mk 84, 2000-pound bombs are used by the Air Force, Navy, and Marines in the low-drag general purpose (LDGP) form. Here a Mk 84 LDGP bomb can be seen under the wing of an F-16 enroute to its target in southern Kuwait. (USAF)

A Mk 84 LDGP bomb is loaded aboard a Marine F/A-18 Hornet during Operation Desert Storm. Again, the Navy/Marine bombs have the thermal protective coating and the two nose stripes. In this photograph, the front yellow stripe is almost obscured by the ground crewman's shoulder. (USAF)

Another Mk 84 LDGP bomb is shown being readied for loading on an aircraft. (USAF)

**Mk 84 AIR (FMU-113 fuse)**
**(fins rotated 45 degrees)**

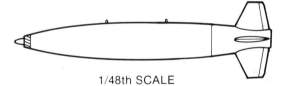

1/72nd SCALE

1/48th SCALE

The Air Force also uses an Air Inflatable Retard (AIR) tail section with its Mk 84 bombs. This tail section is larger in diameter than the one used with the LDGP tail shown above, and it houses a parachute to retard the forward flight of the bomb after it is released from the aircraft. At left is an overall view of a Mk 84 AIR, and at right is a close-up view of the AIR tail section.

(Both Detail & Scale collection)

# CLUSTER BOMB UNITS

## Mk 7 DISPENSER (Mk 20 ROCKEYE II)
(fins rotated 45 degrees)

 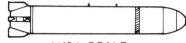

1/72nd SCALE          1/48th SCALE

*The Rockeye family of cluster bombs consists of a Mk 7 dispenser with various submunitions inside. The dispensers are overall gloss white with 2-inch yellow bands about fourteen inches forward of the front lug. The Navy also uses some Mod 6 dispensers with two 1.5-inch yellow bands. These Rockeyes have the rough thermal protective coating to reduce the chances of the weapon exploding in the event of a fire. Rockeyes with both one and two bands can be seen in this photograph. These Rockeyes are CBU-59/B Anti-Personal/Anti-Material (APAM) bombs. They are being readied for loading on Marine A-6E Intruders during Operation Desert Storm.* **(USAF)**

*Another member of the Rockeye series of CBUs is the Mk 20 cluster bomb. It is a Mk 7 dispenser with 247 Mk 118 anti-tank submunitions inside. One of these weapons is shown here being moved to an A-10 Warthog for loading. Three Mk 20s can be seen on the fuselage station of the aircraft.* **(USAF)**

Cluster bomb units (CBU) are a bit more complicated than can be explained in the captions alone, so it is appropriate to provide further information in narrative form. These weapons were used extensively in Desert Storm, and contrary to a report on CNN, cluster bombs are not used only against personnel. Various types of CBUs are effective on concentrations of armor, light skinned vehicles, artillery batteries, and surface-to-air missile sites. It only takes one small hole through the electronic components of a radar to knock it out of action, and a single

submunition from a cluster bomb can blow several holes through a radar. These weapons are also used to disperse anti-personnel and anti-tank mines.

When a person looks at a cluster bomb, all he sees is the dispenser. This is the outer shell or casing of the weapon. Inside are various submunitions, and these in combination with the dispenser determine what type of cluster bomb it is. For example, the SUU-30H dispenser is used for a variety of cluster bombs. When the SUU-30H is filled with 217 BLU-61 fragmenta-

## SUU-30 DISPENSER
(fins rotated 45 degrees)

1/72nd SCALE          1/48th SCALE

*The SUU-30 is another common dispenser which is used with a variety of submunitions to form several different types of cluster bomb units. One of these is the CBU-71/B, four of which can be seen loaded on a BRU under the left wing of an F-111F.*

*(Detail & Scale collection)*

*A different cluster bomb unit that uses the SUU-30 dispenser is the CBU-58, which contains 650 BLU-63 fragmentation bomblets. Two CBU-58s are shown here loaded on an F-4G. CBUs that used the SUU-30 dispenser were overall olive drab with a 1-inch yellow band at the front of the cylindrical portion of the dispenser. Stencilling was white in 5-inch high letters on the top half of the dispenser, and stated the CBU type. "Chock" markings were black.* **(USAF)**

## SUU-64 DISPENSER
**(fins rotated 45 degrees)**

1/72nd SCALE

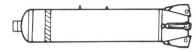

1/48th SCALE

Another dispenser is the SUU-64. The cluster bombs shown in this photograph are CBU-89/B Gator mines. These are SUU-64 dispensers filled with 72 BLU-91 anti-personnel mines and 24 BLU-92 anti-tank mines. These weapons were painted overall olive drab and had a 2-inch yellow band about twelve inches from the front of the cylindrical portion of the dispenser. Gator CBUs had "CBU-89/B" stencilled on the sides of the bombs in 5-inch high yellow letters. *(USAF)*

tion submunitions, it becomes a CBU-52. If it contains 650 BLU-63 fragmentation submunitions, it is a CBU-58. When loaded with 650 BLU-86 fragmentation/incendiary mine submunitions, it is a CBU-71. The SUU-30H is used for both the CBU-89 anti-personnel and CBU-97 anti-armor cluster bomb units.

The Mk 20 Rockeye family of cluster bombs uses two types of dispensers. The Mk 7 dispenser is used by the Air Force, the Navy, and the Marines. The Mk 6 dispenser is similar but has a flame retardant coating to prevent it from "cooking off" in the event of a fire. The Mk 6 dispenser is used only by the Navy and Marines.

Some of the submunitions explode on contact with the target

or the ground, but there are other interesting alternatives. The bomblets in a CBU-71 explode at random times and therefore can serve as mines. The CBU-89 Gator contains a combination of anti-tank and anti-personnel mines. The anti-tank mine senses magnetic disturbances, then it destroys the target with a self-forging warhead. The anti-personnel submunition deploys tripwires which detonate the mine if they are disturbed. Other cluster bomb units have even more complex and exotic submunitions and dispersal systems, but the ones described here and illustrated in the photographs were the main types used during Operation Desert Storm.

## SUU-65 DISPENSER
**(fins rotated 45 degrees)**

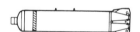

1/72nd SCALE

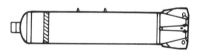

1/48th SCALE

*The SUU-65 dispenser is filled with 202 BLU-97 combined effects munitions (CEM) to form the CBU-87 cluster bomb unit. These two photographs show CBU-87s being loaded on F-111Fs during Operation Desert Storm. These CBUs were painted overall olive drab and had a 2-inch yellow band about twelve inches from the front of the cylindrical portion of the dispenser.* *(Both USAF)*

# SPECIAL PURPOSE BOMBS

### Mk 77, MOD 4 NAPALM

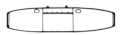

1/72nd SCALE

1/48th SCALE

*The only napalm used during the Gulf War was employed to ignite oil in Iraqi defensive trenches. The Mk 77 napalm canister as shown here was the type of weapon that was used for this purpose. It was unpainted aluminum.*

*(Linn)*

### CBU-55 FUEL AIR EXPLOSIVE
### (fins folded for carriage)

1/72nd SCALE

1/48th SCALE

*CBU-55 and CBU-72 fuel air explosive (FAE) bombs were used in Operation Desert Storm to detonate Iraqi mine fields. They release a fuel vapor into the air and then ignite it. FAEs were overall gloss white with copper colored fuses.*

*(Detail & Scale collection)*

### BLU-82, 15,000 POUND BOMB

1/72nd SCALE

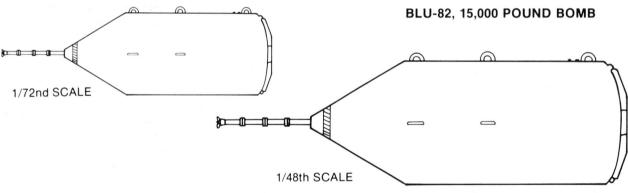

1/48th SCALE

*The BLU-82 blast bomb was the largest bomb used in the Gulf War. At 15,000 pounds, it is the heaviest bomb in the Air Force arsenal. Delivered to its target by an MC-103E Hercules aircraft, it is dropped by shoving it out the rear cargo door along with its cargo pallet. Its descent is slowed by a stabilization parachute, and it is detonated by a M904 fuse attached to the end of a four foot length of pipe. In this photograph, one of these huge bombs is readied for delivery inside an MC-103E. BLU-82s were olive drab or gray, and had a 3-inch yellow band about six inches from the nose. Note the graffiti written all over this particular bomb.* *(Feist via Love)*

# AIR-TO-AIR MISSILES

## AIM-9L & -M SIDEWINDER

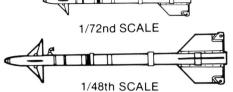

1/72nd SCALE

1/48th SCALE

## AIM-9P-2 SIDEWINDER

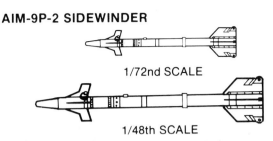

1/72nd SCALE

1/48th SCALE

With one exception, the versions of the Sidewinder air-to-air missile used by U.S. aircraft during Operation Desert Storm were the externally identical AIM-9L and AIM-9M. An AIM-9M is shown on an F-14 Tomcat in the photograph at left. The -M variant was originally a product improvement program for the AIM-9L, and featured closed cycle cooling, infrared countermeasures (IRCM) and background discrimination. It also has a reduced-smoke version of the Mk 36 rocket motor. The one exception occurred only on the first night of the war when F-111Fs carried AIM-9P-3 missiles shoulder mounted on their outboard pylons as seen in the photograph at right. The use of this variant was due to wing clearance problems with the pylon and the larger wings of the -L and -M. The AIM-9L and -Ms had a dark metallic gray guidance section and fins. The fuse sections were silver, and the warhead, rocket motor, and wings were FS 36375 gray. They had a 2-inch yellow band at the back of the warhead and a 3-inch brown band twelve inches from the front of the rocket motor. Most missiles also had a 2-inch red band at the forward hanger where the rocket motor firing impulse entered the missile.

*(Both Detail & Scale collection)*

## AIM-7F & -M SPARROW

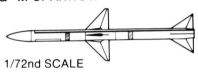

1/72nd SCALE

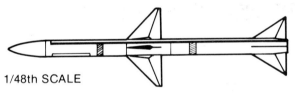

1/48th SCALE

*Right: The AIM-7F and -M variants of the radar guided Sparrow missile were used by F-14 Tomcats, F-15 Eagles, and F/A-18 Hornets during Desert Storm. These two versions of the Sparrow are virtually identical in external appearance. Their missile bodies were painted overall FS 36375 gray and had flat white radomes. The wings and fins were dark metallic gray. A 3-inch yellow band was located at the front of the radome, and a 3-inch brown band was just behind the aft launch lug. This is about 18 inches from the front of the rocket motor.*

## AIM-54C PHOENIX

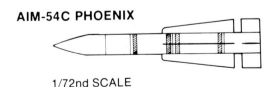

1/72nd SCALE

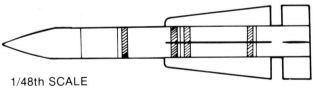

1/48th SCALE

*Left: The AIM-54C Phoenix missile is operationally unique to the F-14 Tomcat. This extremely capable missile has a range many times greater than any other air-to-air missile and can intercept targets that other weapons cannot. Although carried by Tomcats during Operation Desert Storm, no situation arose where the Phoenix was needed, and none were fired. AIM-54Cs were overall FS 36375 gray with flat white radomes. They had 3-inch yellow bands at either end of the warhead and 3-inch brown bands at both ends of the rocket motor.*     *(Detail & Scale collection)*

# AIR-TO-GROUND MISSILES

### AGM-45 SHRIKE

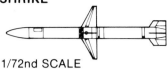

1/72nd SCALE

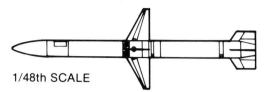

1/48th SCALE

*The AGM-45 Shrike anti-radiation missile was developed and first used during the war in Vietnam. It was also used in limited numbers during Operation Desert Storm. Shrikes were overall gloss white with a 3-inch yellow band at the back of the war-head. A 3-inch black band was painted at the back of the control section, and a 3-inch brown band was at the front of the rocket motor.*

A considerable number of air-to-surface missiles were fired from U.S. aircraft during Operation Desert Storm. Receiving the most publicity was the AGM-88 HARM anti-radiation missile that was used to knock out Iraqi radars that were used to guide surface-to-air missiles. While the F-4G Wild Weasel was the aircraft most closely associated with the HARM, over sixty-one percent of these missiles were delivered by Navy aircraft including the EA-6B Prowler, A-6E Intruder, A-7E Corsair II, and F/A-18 Hornet. F-16Cs from the 52nd TFW also fired HARM missiles during the Gulf War.

Although it received little or no publicity, the AGM-45 Shrike anti-radiation missile was also used in Operation Desert Storm for a short time and in considerably fewer numbers than the AGM-88. The Shrike was developed during the war in Vietnam by the U.S. Navy and is a first generation anti-radiation missile. The second-generation Standard ARM, which was also used in Vietnam, was not employed in Desert Storm.

Approximately 5,500 AGM-65 Maverick missiles were expended during Operation Desert Storm, and about 92 percent of these were fired from A-10 Warthogs. F-16s, A-6Es, and AV-8Bs also fired Mavericks during the war. Although it is a very accurate and lethal weapon, the Maverick demands a heavy workload on the part of the pilot, and therefore is usually not a favorite weapon among pilots of single seat aircraft other than the relatively slow A-10. There are several operational variants of the Maverick, and they can be identified to some degree by their paint schemes. The AGM-65A and -65B are EO guided variants and are painted white. The AGM-65B has the advantage of scene magnification which enables it to be locked on the same target at twice the range of the AGM-65A. These missiles have **SCENE MAG** stencilled on their side. The AGM-65Ds have an imaging infrared (IIR) guidance system and are painted olive drab. AGM-65Es, which are used by the Marines, and the AGM-65F used by the Navy are painted gray. AGM-65Gs have an IIR guidance

### AGM-88 HARM

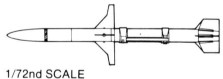

1/72nd SCALE

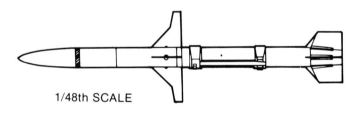

1/48th SCALE

*The AGM-88 HARM is the newest and most capable anti-radiation missile in the U.S. inventory. It was used by Air Force, Navy, and Marines during the Gulf War to suppress radar guided surface-to-air missile systems. At left is a HARM on the inboard right wing pylon of an F-4G Wild Weasel, and at right is another AGM-88 on the inboard left wing station of an EA-6B Prowler. HARMs were overall flat white with a 2-inch yellow band at the front of the warhead. A 2-inch brown band circled the missile at the front of the rocket motor.*

*(Left USAF, right Official U.S. Navy Photograph by LT Gerald Parsons)*

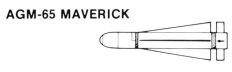

1/72nd SCALE

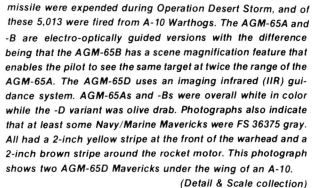

1/48th SCALE

*Left: Over 5,500 AGM-65A, -B, and -D variants of the Maverick missile were expended during Operation Desert Storm, and of these 5,013 were fired from A-10 Warthogs. The AGM-65A and -B are electro-optically guided versions with the difference being that the AGM-65B has a scene magnification feature that enables the pilot to see the same target at twice the range of the AGM-65A. The AGM-65D uses an imaging infrared (IIR) guidance system. AGM-65As and -Bs were overall white in color while the -D variant was olive drab. Photographs also indicate that at least some Navy/Marine Mavericks were FS 36375 gray. All had a 2-inch yellow stripe at the front of the warhead and a 2-inch brown stripe around the rocket motor. This photograph shows two AGM-65D Mavericks under the wing of an A-10.*

*(Detail & Scale collection)*

system, but their warhead is larger than earlier versions. Those used by the USAF are olive drab, while the ones in the Navy's inventory are gray.

Making its combat debut during Operation Desert Storm was the AGM-84E SLAM or Standoff Land Attack Missile. This missile was actually still in development, so only seven were fired during the Gulf War. The SLAM is a lengthened AGM-84D Harpoon missile. It receives data from Global Positioning System (GPS) satellites and uses the Maverick's imaging infrared (IIR) seeker for terminal guidance. A Walleye Phase II command receiver and video transmitter provide the data link between the controlling aircraft and the missile. During its first use in combat, two SLAMs were fired at an Iraqi power station. The first blew a hole in the side of the structure, and the second SLAM went through the hole to detonate inside and destroy the station. These SLAMs were launched from A-6Es of VA-75 assigned to

Carrier Air Wing Three aboard the USS JOHN F. KENNEDY. They were guided to their targets by an A-7E, also from the KENNEDY.

Although it was used only once by one type of aircraft during Operation Desert Storm, another air-to-surface missile deserves mention here. One year after the opening night of Operation Desert Storm, the Air Force released information confirming that B-52Gs from Barksdale AFB had fired thirty-five conventionally armed AGM-86C cruise missiles during the first night of the war. These air-launched cruise missiles (ALCM) were targeted against high-priority targets in Iraq, and supplemented the Tomahawk cruise missiles that were launched from ships that same night. Because of the fact that this missile was used only one time and only by the B-52G, coverage of the ALCM can be found with the information about the B-52G that appears on pages 44 and 45.

## AGM-84E SLAM (fins rotated 45 degrees)

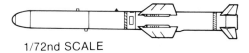

1/72nd SCALE

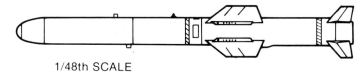

1/48th SCALE

*The SLAM (Standoff Land Attack Missile) was still in development during Operation Desert Storm, and only seven were launched during the war. The SLAM combines the airframe, propulsion, and control systems of the AGM-84 Harpoon missile with the AGM-65D Maverick's infrared seeker. It is controlled from the launching aircraft or from a second aircraft through the Walleye data-link pod. The first launch of the SLAM during the war was made from an A-6E of VA-75 assigned to the USS JOHN F. KENNEDY. It was controlled by an A-7E Corsair II from the same carrier. Two SLAMs can be seen beneath the wings of this A-6E Intruder. (McDonnell Douglas)*

# ECM PODS

### ALQ-119(V)-15 ECM POD

Although they are not weapons nor are they delivered against enemy targets, ECM pods are important external stores found on many Air Force aircraft. They are designed to deceive enemy radars and prevent them from getting accurate information about the aircraft. This is the ALQ-119 long ECM pod, which was used in the greatest numbers during the Gulf War. ALQ-119 ECM pods were seen in several color schemes. A few were still white with black radomes, but most were olive drab with black radomes. Others were FS 36375 gray with olive drab radomes, and a small number of pods were a combination of gray and olive drab.

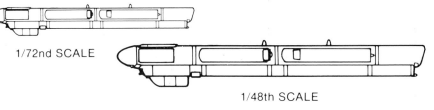

1/72nd SCALE

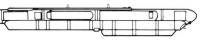

1/48th SCALE

### ALQ-184(V)-1 ECM POD

The ALQ-184 long ECM pod is very similar to the ALQ-119 shown above, however, its gondola is considerably longer. This is the portion of the pod that hangs down near the forward end. The ALQ-184 long pod was used only by F-4G Wild Weasel aircraft from the 35th Tactical Fighter Wing. It was carried in the forward left Sparrow missile bay as shown in this photograph. The larger gondola is clearly visible in this view. ALQ-184 pods were overall FS 36270 gray.

(Bell)

1/72nd SCALE

1/48th SCALE

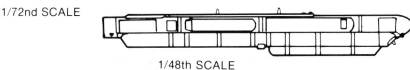

### ALQ-131 DEEP ECM POD

1/72nd SCALE        1/48th SCALE

The ALQ-131 deep ECM pod was widely used, being carried on many F-16s and 52nd TFW F-4Gs. They were seen in the white, gray, and olive drab paint schemes described for the ALQ-119 above.    (Bell)

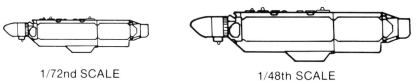

### ALQ-131 SHALLOW ECM POD

1/72nd SCALE        1/48th SCALE

The ALQ-131 shallow ECM pod was unique to the F-111, and was usually carried on the aft fuselage station between the strakes. The pod shown in this photograph is olive drab with a white radome, but other pods had black radomes.

(Detail & Scale collection)

# MODELERS SECTION
## AIRCRAFT KITS

*General Note: In each of the previous volumes of the Detail & Scale Series, the Modelers Section has contained detailed reviews of the model kits for the specific aircraft or ship that was covered by that particular book. Since this publication covers sixteen different aircraft types, it is not possible to follow that format. Instead we are providing information about which kits of these aircraft are the best ones for modelers to use when building replicas in each of the major or standard modeling scales. These are 1/144th, 1/72nd, 1/48th and 1/32nd scales. To obtain this information, we formed a panel of experienced modelers who are also knowledgeable about the actual aircraft. The members of the panel were given several weeks to come up with their recommendations independently, then they turned in their findings in writing on specially prepared forms. Of primary concern was the accuracy of the kit, but other factors such as price, fit, and ease of assembly were also considered. What follows is a consensus of the reports filed by our panel. The aircraft are presented in the same order in which they are covered in this publication.*

*For a more detailed look at the available kits of each type of aircraft, modelers should refer to the specific volume in the Detail & Scale Series that covers the individual aircraft in question. All of the aircraft have been the subject of previous Detail & Scale titles except for the EA-6B Prowler and the F-117A Night Hawk.*

*All information provided in this part of the Modelers Section, as well as the parts on the armament and decals that follow, was current as of February 1993, which was the press time for this book.*

### F-15C Eagle

In 1/144th scale, DML makes the best F-15C, and modelers will want to look for kit 4512. As an alternative, kit 1029 from LS is also quite good. As is the case with most kits in this tiny scale, the interiors are lacking detail. In the DML kits, a part for the interior is usually provided with seats and pilots that look less like people and more like droids from the movie **Star Wars.** We recommend scratchbuilding basic interiors or replacing the kit parts with 1/144th scale ejection seats from Commander Series Models.

Hasegawa's kit K25 gets the nod as the best of the F-15Cs in 1/72nd scale, however, this model is considerably overpriced in our estimation. Another quality kit in this scale is the one from ESCI/ERTL. It is beautifully engraved and has excellent fit. Of equal value is Minicraft's kit number 2108.

The unanimous choice in 1/48th scale is Hasegawa's kit P10. But again this is a very expensive model. Minicraft's kit 1685 is also quite good for a lot less money, and so is Monogram's kit 5823. Monogram's Eagle suffers from raised panel lines, but it is a very accurate model. We believe that the Minicraft and Monogram kits are the better value for the money, and will be more than adequate in quality for most modelers.

Only one F-15C has been released in 1/32nd scale, and it is Revell's kit 4800. It is no longer in production, but it can be found at swap meets and modeler's conventions. It is a good value for the money and can be built into an impressive and accurate model. Hopefully, it will be reissued.

### F-15E Strike Eagle

With the exception of the DML 1/144th scale kit, all models of the Strike Eagle represent the F-15E prototype with varying degrees of updates. None represents the production aircraft,

and any modeler building in any scale other then 1/144th will have a lot of work to do in the form of updating and correcting in order to finish with an up-to-date F-15E. Considering how well the model manufacturers have kept up with the many changes made to the F-16, F/A-18, and other aircraft, it is difficult to understand why the modeling community still does not have an accurate model of this important aircraft in 1/72nd, 1/48th, and 1/32nd scales.

DML's kit 4543 of the F-15E is the only accurate model of a production Strike Eagle, and it is the only kit to choose in this scale. Earlier releases by DML, including kit 4002 and double kit 4022, did not have the pylons or weapons for the conformal fuel tanks.

In 1/72nd scale, Hasegawa's kit KT1 or K27 is rated the best, but kit 2110 from Minicraft is also a good place to start at less than half the price. But whichever kit is chosen, the modeler will have a lot of work to do. Changes not usually seen in the Strike Eagle kits include the addition of pylons on the conformal fuel pallets and a change to the tail-mounted antenna on the fairing just to the right of the engines. The F-15E has a stronger main gear with wider tires, and the gear doors are bulged to accommodate the wider wheels and tires. The place where the ammunition is loaded into the gun is completely different from other Eagles, and the ejection seats have canopy breakers. Some or all of these features are missing from the kits and will have to be added as required in order to represent the F-15E production aircraft.

In 1/48th scale the story is the same. We suggest starting with Minicraft kit number 1687, because it comes closer to a production Strike Eagle than any of the other kits in this scale. But there will still be a lot of updating and correcting to do. There are two side pylons for each of the conformal fuel pallets, but there should be three. The other kits have none. Minicraft includes an ASAT missile, but the F-15E does not carry this weapon.

The only Strike Eagle available in 1/32nd scale is Revell's kit 4719. It is no longer in production, and it too represents the prototype aircraft. With a lot of work, it can be turned into an excellent model of a production aircraft, but it will take a very skilled and patient modeler to do so.

*Master modeler John Ficklen used the Revell 1/32nd scale Strike Eagle to build this excellent model of an F-15E from the 4th TFW during Operation Desert Storm. The Revell kit, as well as most others of the Strike Eagle, represents the F-15E prototype. Therefore, much extra work is required in the form of detailing and updating to produce an accurate production version of the Strike Eagle.*

### F-16A Fighting Falcon

The DML 1/144th scale F-16 kits all have optional vertical tails to allow them to be built as either an F-16A or an F-16C. However, only kit 9905 has the smaller horizontal stabilizers used on the early Blocks 5 and 10 aircraft. Since the only F-16As used in Operation Desert Storm were these early versions that were flown by the South Carolina and New York Air National Guards, this kit is the best choice. It also has New York's markings as used in the Gulf War as well as the GPU-5, 30-mm gun pod which that unit used for one day during the war. However, this kit also has the flat engine inlet that is common to all DML 1/144th scale F-16s.

In 1/72nd scale we recommend the Hasegawa F-16A in kit number 601. The one problem is that it only has the larger horizontal stabilizers of the later aircraft, so these will have to be modified. An option would be to make new stabilizers from plastic card, or the modeler could use the earlier stabilizers that are included in other kits of the F-16A. Fujimi kit number 7AE2 is also a good kit in this scale but would require the same change to the horizontal stabilizers. F-16As from Testors and ERTL are also good models.

In 1/48th scale Hasegawa's kit number V1 is the best, but it requires the change to the horizontal tail, as does kit number 1688 from Minicraft. While the Hasegawa kit is a little better, the Minicraft model is the best value for the money. Monogram's early kit of the F-16A would not require any change to the horizontal tail surfaces, and it also builds up into a nice model.

Hasegawa's F-16s in 1/32nd scale are all very expensive, but kit S25 is certainly the best in this scale if money is no object. Kits S20 and S26 are also F-16As, and all three go for over $50.00. A less expensive way to go is to take Revell's kit number 4735 and convert it back to an F-16A. It will take a little time, but it would be a relatively simple task that would save a lot of money. If one can be found at a swap meet, the original Revell issue in this scale was kit number 4701. It represented an early F-16A and would require no backdating.

*The author used the old Revell kit (H-222) in 1/72nd scale to build this F-16A in the markings used by New York's Air National Guard during Operation Desert Storm.*

### F-16C Fighting Falcon

There are dozens of good kits of the F-16 in every conceivable scale. In 1/144th scale the best ones are from DML. This company has several issues of the F-16C including kit numbers 4511 and 4545. They are accurate little models except for the engine air inlet which is squashed almost flat. It is so out of shape that it must be completely rebuilt by the modeler. As an alternative, inlets from the LS or Revell 1/144th scale F-16s could be used.

In 1/72nd scale, the best kit is from Hasegawa. Kit 603 builds

*The Fujimi kit of the F-16C in 1/72nd scale builds up into an accurate model of the Fighting Falcon.*

up into a super model, but like other models from Hasegawa, this kit is rather expensive. Another good choice is the kit from Fujimi numbered G-20.

In 1/48th scale, Hasegawa has several excellent kits. These include V8, which is the most up-to-date and has LANTIRN pods. V4 is a Block 30 aircraft with the GE F110 engine, and V3 has the Pratt & Whitney engine. Again, these kits are very expensive, and there is a good alternative. Minicraft kit 1688 can be built as either an F-16A or F-16C, and it costs about six dollars less than the Hasegawa kits.

In 1/32nd scale, Hasegawa's kit S25 is clearly the best, but with a retail price of $68.00, many modelers will opt for Revell's kit 4735 which sells for less than $18.00. It is not as good as the Hasegawa model, but it is still a good kit. We do not think that the Hasegawa kit is $50.00 better, but that choice is up to the individual modeler.

### F-4G Wild Weasel

No kits of the F-4G exist in 1/144th scale, however, a conversion from an F-4E would be a relatively simple matter. The most difficult part would be changing the non-slatted wing to the slatted type. Start with the LS F-4E in kit number 1034, Revell's kit number 4768, or the Hobbycraft kit 1006.

Hasegawa's kit KA8 is the best model in 1/72nd scale, but Fujimi's kit 16006 is not far behind and costs less. The Testors/Italeri kit 684 is an even less expensive alternative that is also worth considering.

In 1/48th scale Hasegawa again has the best model in kit P4. Kits 572 and 583 from Testors/Italeri are the only other real choices. These kits are fairly accurate in outline, but lack the detailing of the more expensive Hasegawa kit.

There are no kits of the F-4G in 1/32nd scale, but a conversion could be done from one of Revell's old F-4E kits. These are now out of production, and they had a lot of problems. Doing a conversion would not only involve making all of the necessary changes, but it would also require doing a lot of kit correcting too. Such a project would undoubtedly provide many hours of modeling pleasure!

### RF-4C Phantom II

There are no recon Phantoms in 1/144th scale, but a conversion from the LS, Revell, or Hobbycraft F-4E kits mentioned above would be even easier than doing an F-4G. In 1/72nd scale, Hasegawa kit KA10 is the best, but ESCI/ERTL's kit 9029 is also quite good, as is kit G-14 from Fujimi. Testors/Italeri's kit 682 can also be built into a nice model, but comes up short on cockpit detailing.

The only choice the modeler really has in 1/48th scale is

*This RF-4C was built by the author using the 1/72nd scale Hasegawa kit and RepliScale decals.*

Testors kit 585. This is a pretty good kit as far as accuracy of outline and shape is concerned, but the detailing in the cockpit leaves a bit to be desired. In 1/32nd scale, Revell's RF-4B kit 4768 can be converted to an RF-4C, but again the model itself needs a lot of work as far as kit correcting goes. At this time, there is no other way to build an RF-4C in this large scale.

### F-111E Aardvark

The only kits of the F-111E in 1/144th scale are Crown's kit 4, and Otaki's kit 2-21, which was re-released by AMT/ERTL as kit 8857. Of these the AMT/ERTL kit is the best. All of these kits represent an F-111E. In 1/72nd scale the excellent Hasegawa kit K36 is the choice. This is one case where the extra money paid for the Hasegawa model is well worth it over any other choice. Models of the F-111 from other kit manufacturers are much older and lack the accuracy and detail of the Hasegawa kit.

In 1/48th scale the only kit to consider is Minicraft's kit 1689. Although it has a few inaccuracies, it is far and away the best choice. There are no kits of the F-111E in 1/32nd scale.

### F-111F Aardvark

No kits of the F-111F exist in 1/144th scale, and converting an Otaki or AMT/ERTL F-111E to a Pave Tack F-111F would be rather tedious. However, it is the only way to build a 1/144th scale model of this aircraft that played such an important role in Operation Desert Storm. Hopefully, DML will soon add quality F-111 kits to its excellent line of 1/144th scale models.

In 1/72nd scale, the only real choice is Hasegawa kit K34. It is expensive, but it is really the only accurate F-111F on the market,

*Marc Schachter of San Diego, California, used the Hasegawa 1/72nd scale F-111F to build this extensively detailed F-111F. It represents the wing commander's aircraft from the 48th TFW, and it won the Detail & Scale Special Award for the best detailed aircraft model at the 1991 IPMS National Convention in St. Louis, Missouri.*

*The 1/48th scale Minicraft F-111F was used by Frank Mitchell to build this model of an aircraft from the 48th Tactical Fighter Wing. External fuel tanks were not carried during Desert Storm.*

and it has the Pave Tack system. In 1/48th scale, the Minicraft kit 1679 is the place to start. The kit does not have the Pave Tack pod, and a few inaccuracies will need to be corrected. See Detail & Scale Volume 4 (Revised Edition) for a complete explanation of what needs to be done. There are no F-111F kits in 1/32nd scale.

### EF-111A Raven

When it comes to building models of the EF-111A, the story is about the same as it is for the F-111E and F-111F. In 1/144th scale, the only way to build a Raven is to convert an Otaki or AMT/ERTL kit. This would undoubtedly be quite involved, but it seems like it would be a very interesting project. Revell of Germany's EA-6B Prowler could be cannibalized for some of the parts.

In 1/72nd scale there are three kits of the EF-111A available, and all can be used to build excellent models. Hasegawa's kit KT3 is rated the best, and Monogram's kit 5435 is a close second with a more reasonable price tag. Also available is the ESCI/ERTL kit 8831.

Minicraft's kit 1676 is the only EF-111A available in 1/48th scale, and there are no models of the Raven in 1/32nd scale.

### F-117A Nighthawk

There has been a lot of controversy about the F-117A kits, and the earliest ones suffer some real accuracy problems. In 1/144th scale, DML's "revised tooling" kit 9904 is clearly the best. In 1/72nd scale, the nod goes to Minicraft's kit 2107, but Revell's revised kit 4460 is worth considering as well.

*DML's kit number 9904 is an excellent model of the F-117A in 1/144th scale.*

The best kit in 1/48th scale is Monogram's kit 5834, and the second choice is Testors kit 577. In 1/32nd scale, the only model that is available is kit 570 from Testors. However, it has a number of major accuracy problems that will take a lot of time and work to correct. The modeler should get a lot of good reference material if he is going to tackle this one.

### F-14A Tomcat

There are many kits of the Tomcat available, and several of them are quite good. For the F-14A, we recommend the LS kits in 1/144th scale, several of which were released. The most recent of these is kit number 1067. However, DML's F-14A kits are equally as good, and we recommend them as well. In 1/72nd scale, Hasegawa's kit K38 is the best, but we can also recommend a number of other kits in this scale. These include Minicraft kit 1676, Fujimi kit 28003, and ESCI/ERTL kit 9054. Hasegawa's kit SP44 is the best in 1/48th scale, but the price is quite high. Alternatives worth considering are Monogram's kit 5803 and Minicraft's kit 1679.

Tamiya's kit 6301 was selected as the best Tomcat in 1/32nd scale, but only by a very small margin. In some respects it is the best, but in others Revell's kit 4770 is better. Either can be built up into an impressive model, but they both will take a lot of work.

*The Minicraft 1/48th scale F-14 is an excellent kit for the money. This model was built by Scott Hackney of Omaha, Nebraska, to represent a Tomcat from VF-32 and the USS JOHN F. KENNEDY during Operation Desert Storm.*

### F-14A+ Tomcat

The DML 1/144th scale kits are better than the LS models for this updated Tomcat. DML kit 4529 is the best selection, but it has also been released with other kit numbers. In 1/72nd scale, Hasegawa's kit SP-2 has all of the necessary updates, and it is truly excellent. Fujimi also makes a fine F-14A+ as kit 35117, but its cost is $40.00. A simplified version is Fujimi kit 28002, and its price is $28.00. But that is still more than the $23.00 price of kit SP-2 from Hasegawa. The only way to avoid paying these rather high prices for a 1/72nd scale fighter is to use Testors' kit 649 or convert the Monogram or Minicraft kits to an F-14A+.

In 1/48th scale, we recommend Hasegawa kits SP8 or 7023. These cost $56.00, which is quite high for a 1/48th scale fighter, but the only other way to build an F-14A+ in this scale is to convert a basic F-14A kit.

In 1/32nd scale there is no kit of the F-14A+, so the modeler must update either the Tamiya or Revell kit.

### F/A-18 Hornet

DML kit 4513 and its sister releases are the best, but LS kit 1030 is also recommended. In 1/72nd scale, Hasegawa's kit ET1 is the choice of our panel, and it has all of the changes necessary to build an accurate and up-to-date F/A-18C. In 1/48th scale

*Hasegawa's kit number ET 1 is the best and most up-to-date F/A-18 Hornet in 1/72nd scale.*

*Darrell Cochran of Pampa, Texas, used the Monogram 1/48th scale F/A-18 Hornet to build this model. Although the Hasegawa 1/48th scale Hornet is a better kit, its very high price tag makes this Monogram release the better choice in most cases.*

Hasegawa kit SP68 is truly excellent, but it is considered to be overpriced at $78.00. Monogram's kit 5807 lists for only $11.15, and although the modeler will have to scratchbuild some of the updates to build an F/A-18C, it is well worth the savings of some $67.00. Testors kit 579 is also worth consideration. The choice will be dictated by the depth of the modeler's wallet.

Hasegawa and Revell both issued 1/32nd scale kits of the Hornet prototype, but neither are still in production. The better choice is Hasegawa kit S23, but the modeler should refer to Detail & Scale Volume 6 for information about the major surgery that is required to turn this into a production aircraft.

### A-6E Intruder

DML kits of the A-6E in 1/144th scale are clearly the best, and several releases have been made with different decals. The Fujimi kit number 346, which has also been released by Testors, was the choice in 1/72nd scale. The Revell/ACE kit 4365 and the Hasegawa kit 709 are good, but really are not up to the standards of the Fujimi/Testors models.

In 1/48th scale, Revell's kit number 4578 is clearly superior to the Fujimi and Testors releases. There is no A-6E in 1/32nd scale.

### EA-6B Prowler

Revell of Germany offers the only EA-6B in 1/144th scale, and its kit number is 4055. It would be very nice to see Revell/USA make this model easier to obtain in the United States. In 1/72nd scale, there are a few more choices, and Hasegawa's kit K14 is the best. Hobbycraft's kits 1337 and 1381 can also be built up into nice models.

In 1/48th scale, Monogram's kit 5611 is clearly superior to the older and discontinued Airfix model which was also released by

# TABULAR SUMMARY OF THE BEST MODEL KITS OF U.S. AIRCRAFT USED IN OPERATION DESERT STORM

| AIRCRAFT TYPE | 1/144th SCALE | 1/72nd SCALE | 1/48th SCALE | 1/32nd SCALE |
|---|---|---|---|---|
| F-15C | DML 4512 | Hasegawa K25 | Hasegawa P10 | Revell 4800 * |
| F-15E | DML 4534 | Hasegawa KT1 | Minicraft 1687 | Revell 4719 * |
| F-16C | DML 4535 | Hasegawa 603 | Hasegawa V8 | Hasegawa S25 |
| F-16A | DML 9905 | Hasegawa 601 | Hasegawa V1 | Hasegawa S25 |
| F-4G | NONE ** | Hasegawa KA8 | Hasegawa P4 | NONE ** |
| RF-4C | NONE ** | Hasegawa KA10 | Testors 582 | Revell 4768 |
| F-111E | AMT/ERTL 8857 | Hasegawa K36 | Minicraft 1689 | NONE |
| F-111F | NONE ** | Hasegawa K34 | Minicraft 1675 | NONE |
| EF-111A | NONE ** | Hasegawa KT3 | Minicraft 1676 | NONE |
| F-117A | DML 9904 | Minicraft 2107 | Monogram 5834 | Testors 570 |
| F-14A | LS 1067 | Hasegawa K38 | Hasegawa SP44 | Tamiya 6301 |
| F-14A+ | DML 4529 | Hasegawa SP2 | Hasegawa SP8 | NONE ** |
| F/A-18 | DML 4513 | Hasegawa ET1 | Hasegawa SP68 | Hasegawa S23 |
| A-6E | DML 4516 | Fujimi 346 | Revell 4578 | NONE |
| EA-6B | Revell 4055 | Hasegawa K14 | Monogram 5611 | NONE |
| A-7E | NONE | Fujimi 35121 | Hasegawa P14 | NONE |
| AV-8B | DML 4520 | Testors 688 | Monogram 5448 | NONE |
| A-10 | DML 4548 | Hasegawa K17 | Monogram 5505 | NONE |
| B-52G | Revell 4583 | NONE ** | NONE | NONE |

This table indicates the **BEST** model in each of the major modeling scales for all of the aircraft covered in this publication. The determination was made based solely on the quality of the kit and does not include subjective factors such as the cost of the kit. In many cases quality "second choice" kits are also available at a much lower price. This is particularly true where Hasegawa kits are listed as the best. These kits are often very expensive.

The choice for **BEST** model as indicated in this table is a consensus made by a panel of experienced modelers who are also knowledgeable about the actual aircraft.

In many cases the kits listed in this table have also been released under other kit numbers in addition to those shown above.

Some of the kits listed are the **ONLY** kit available of the aircraft in a given scale. In such cases the quality of these kits varies considerably. Modelers should refer to the narrative for more information on these kits with respect to quality and availability.

Kits marked with an asterisk (*) are no longer in production but might be obtained from collectors. Kits which are no longer commercially available are listed as the **BEST** choice only when no other kit of the given aircraft exists in that scale.

When the word NONE is followed by two asterisks (**), a model can be built in the scale indicated by doing a conversion to a kit of a different variant of the aircraft. Refer to the text for information about the necessary conversion.

---

MPC. There are no Prowler kits in 1/32nd scale.

*The 1/48th scale Airfix kit of the EA-6B Prowler was used by Bobby Winnett of Warrior, Alabama, to build this model.*

### A-7E Corsair II

Along with the fact that there are no good kits of many of the F-4 Phantom II variants in 1/144th scale, the lack of any kits at all of the A-7 Corsair II in this scale is one of the major puzzles in this hobby. Perhaps a kit manufacturer will recognize this and add a series of all A-7 variants to the line of 1/144th scale models currently available.

In 1/72nd scale, there are many choices, but Fujimi's kit 35121 is certainly the best. This kit was also released by Testors as kit 340. Excellent models can also be built from the ESCI/ERTL kit 9064, the ACE kit number 1200, and Airfix kit 3016. Hasegawa's kit P14 is the best of the 1/48th scale kits, and the ESCI/ERTL kit 8861 is rated second. There are no injection molded A-7 kits in 1/32nd scale.

### AV-8B Harrier II

DML's kit 4520 is the only choice in 1/144th scale, and this is a good model. Our panel selected the Testors/Italeri kit number

688 as the best in 1/72nd scale but also gave good marks to ESCI/ERTL kit 9060. Monogram's kit 5448 is the only one in 1/48th scale, and it is a very nice model. There are no AV-8B kits in 1/32nd scale.

### A-10 Thunderbolt II

Kit 4548 and its sister release 4549 from DML are the best A-10s in 1/144th scale. These kits even have basic cockpit interiors which is a nice new feature in this small scale. We hope to see more of it. In 1/72nd scale, we recommend Hasegawa's kit K17 by the smallest of margins over Minicraft's excellent 1652. The nod goes to the Hasegawa kit simply because it has the updates made to the actual aircraft, but the Minicraft kit has engraved panel lines. Monogram's kit 3430 is also worth consideration, but it has some real fit problems.

Monogram's kit 5505 was chosen as the best of the 1/48th scale Warthogs, but Tamiya kit 61023 is also quite good. Its main problem is that it is of an early production aircraft and lacks many of the newer features found on the Monogram kit. There is no kit of the A-10 available in 1/32nd scale.

### B-52G Stratofortress

The only kit of the B-52G in any of the major modeling scales is Revell's kit 4583 in 1/144th scale. It is superb, but in order to build an aircraft from Desert Storm, the ordnance will have to be changed. Be ready to buy a lot of LS weapons sets to get enough M117, 750-pound bombs. Even then, the four fins will have to be

*Jerry Taylor of Oklahoma City built this B-52G using the Revell 1/144th scale kit.*

changed on every bomb. Perhaps it would be best just to leave the aircraft unarmed! DML released a B-52G in 1/200th scale that was also marketed by Testors, but this "off-scale" kit will not fit into many collections. There are relatively few aircraft kits in this scale.

The Monogram B-52D kit 5709 in 1/72nd scale can be combined with DB Models' conversion kit to build a B-52G if the modeler is willing to do a lot of work. See Detail & Scale Volume 27 for information about this conversion.

# ARMAMENT IN SCALE

*General Note: This part of the Modelers Section is intended to provide helpful information about how the modeler might construct accurate representations of externally carried weapons and ECM pods that are not generally available in kit form. It is unfortunate and hard to believe that the model manufacturers have not yet come forward with new weapons sets or aircraft kits that include the latest Paveway II laser guided bombs and other recently developed armament that made the headlines during Operation Desert Storm. Therefore, the modeler must convert these from other weapons or build them from scratch.*

*Even if a weapon must be built entirely from scratch, this is often not too difficult and is within the ability of most average modelers. All that is generally required is some plastic rod or sprue in varying diameters and some thin plastic card stock. Whether doing a conversion or building from scratch, the modeler should refer to the scale drawings that are included in this publication.*

*With two exceptions we are not including information about standard bombs, air-to-air missiles, or air-to-ground missiles. For the most part, these weapons are readily available in many aircraft kits and weapons sets, and they are very easy to find. The two exceptions are the Mk 82 and Mk 84 AIR standard bombs and the SLAM air-to-surface missile. Appropriate comments are included for these weapons.*

*We are also not covering napalm canisters, the fuel air explosive bomb, or the BLU-82 bomb, since these were used very sparingly and on only one or two types of aircraft. Instead, we are limiting our discussion primarily to the precision guided munitions that played such an important role in Operation Desert Storm. Comments are also included for cluster bombs which were used in large numbers, and for two ECM pods that cannot be found in kits.*

*LS has released these two kits of weapons for 1/144th scale models. Although they lack the newer precision guided munitions used in the Gulf War, they will be valuable to any modeler who builds in this scale.*

Hasegawa has issued several weapons sets in 1/72nd scale. These four kits will be of particular interest to modelers, because they include a wide variety of weapons. Some of these can be used as a basis for conversions to represent the newer precision guided munitions that were used in Operation Desert Storm.

These three kits from Hasegawa are in 1/48th scale, and they provide numerous external stores in this popular scale. Like other weapons kits, they lack the newer laser guided bombs used in the Gulf War.

## LASER GUIDED BOMBS

### GBU-10C, -D, & -E Paveway II

In most cases the GBU-10 is represented in kit form only in its earlier Paveway I versions which were not used in Operation Desert Storm. The Paveway I bombs had wing sections with fixed wings, while the Paveway II bombs that were used in the Gulf have wing sections with wings that pop out or deploy when the weapon is dropped. In the Minicraft and Revell 1/72nd models of the F-117A, the laser guided bombs that are included are very close representations of the GBU-10C, -D, and -E. The wing sections really do not truly represent the pop-out wings, but they are close and could be easily modified. Also in 1/72nd scale, the Airfix RAF/NATO weapons kit number 05041 has a British CPU-123 laser guided bomb. Its guidance and wing sections are very similar to those used on the GBU-10 Paveway II bombs. These could prove helpful to the modeler in converting GBU-10 Paveway I versions to Paveway II bombs.

The earlier Paveway I versions are available in 1/144th, 1/72nd, and 1/48th scales. These are in several aircraft kits in 1/72nd and 1/48th scales, but the best representations are found in the various weapons sets. GBU-10 Paveway I laser guided bombs can be found in LS kit number S202 in 1/144th scale, Hasegawa weapons set X72-2 and Testors NATO aircraft armament kit number 860 in 1/72nd scale, and in Hasegawa weapons set X48-2 in 1/48th scale. GBU-10 Paveway I guided bombs can also be found in Testors' models of the F-117A in 1/72nd, 1/48th, and 1/32nd scales where they are identified on the instructions simply as Mk 84 laser guided bombs. Starting with these models of the GBU-10 Paveway I, the modeler can remove the guidance fins and the wing sections. Then by using plastic card, the correct fins and wing sections can be added to convert the weapon to the GBU-10C, -D, or -E. In 1/32nd scale, the modeler can begin with the GBU-10 Paveway I LGBs in the Hasegawa F-16 kits or the Testors F-117A and modify the guidance fins and the tail sections in the same manner as for the smaller scales. Refer to the drawings on page 46 for reference.

### GBU-10G, -H, & -J Paveway II

There are no models of these variants of the GBU-10 Paveway II bomb in any scale. However, the BLU-109 or I-2000 warhead used for these weapons is basically cylindrical in shape and is therefore easy to make from a plastic rod or dowel. The guidance section can be modified from the earlier GBU-10 models listed above, or it can be scratchbuilt. The wing section will have to be built from scratch, but again this should not prove too difficult for the experienced modeler.

In 1/144th scale, the modeler can take the two GBU-27As from DML kit number 9904 of the F-117A and cut off the guidance section. The guidance section from a GBU-10 from the LS kit number S202 could then be added. Drawings of the GBU-10G, -H, & -J are on page 46.

### GBU-12B, -C, & -D Paveway II

As with the GBU-10, the GBU-12 LGBs available in kit form represent the older Paveway I versions. Again, the easiest way to build the Paveway II variants used in the Gulf War is to start with one of the older versions and modify the guidance fins and tail sections using the drawings on page 46 for reference. GBU-12 Paveway I bombs can be found in LS kit number S202 in 1/144th scale, Hasegawa kit number X72-2 and Testors kit number 860 in 1/72nd scale, and Hasegawa kit number X48-2 in 1/48th scale. There are no models of GBU-12s in 1/32nd scale. Therefore, the modeler should begin with a basic 500-pound bomb from one of several 1/32nd scale kits. He must then scratchbuild the guidance and wing sections from plastic rod, sprue, and card stock. Scale drawings for the GBU-12 are also on page 46.

### GBU-16A & -B Paveway II and AGM-123A Skipper

We have been unable to find any version of the GBU-16 in kit form. Therefore, regardless of scale, the modeler should start with a Mk 83, 1000-pound bomb and add the guidance and wing sections from scratch. Mk 83s are included in LS weapons kit number S201 in 1/144th scale, Hasegawa kit number X72-1 in 1/72nd scale. Hasegawa weapons set X48-1 in 1/48th scale, and

the Hasegawa F-5E kit in 1/32nd scale.

To build the AGM-123A Skipper, the modeler needs only to scratchbuild a small rocket motor and add it to the GBU-16A. This can be made from a plastic rod or sprue. Drawings for these weapons are on page 47.

### GBU-24 Paveway III

No version of the GBU-24 exists in kit form. The modeler should start with a basic Mk 84, 2000-pound bomb in the desired scale, then build the guidance and wing sections from scratch. The guidance section will be a little easier than with other laser guided bombs because it is cylindrical in shape and has a rounded nose. However, the tail section with its offset wings will be considerably more challenging. The scale drawings of the GBU-24 are on page 48.

### GBU-24A Paveway III

Again, there is no model of this weapon in any scale, and building one from scratch will undoubtedly prove to be the most difficult of any of the guided bombs. It will be particularly hard to represent the hardback adapter and the sawtooth area of the tail section where it fits on to the BLU-109 warhead. In 1/144th scale, the modeler could use the GBU-27As found in DML kit number 9904 of the F-117A. In this small scale it would be relatively simple to add the turtleback and change the tail section to represent the GBU-24A. Refer to the drawings on page 48.

### GBU-27 Paveway III

No model of the GBU-27 is available in kit form. The easiest way to make one is to use the GBU-27A laser guided bombs that are provided in DML kit 9904 of the F-117A. Cut the guidance and wing sections off of the bombs from this kit and attach them to a Mk 84 bomb body from another 1/144th scale kit or the LS weapons set S201. It will be necessary to remove the standard tail section from the Mk 84 before adding the GBU-27 tail section.

In the other modeling scales, the modeler must also start with a Mk 84 bomb and scratchbuild the guidance and wing sections. For the modeler with more money than time, it is possible to begin with the laser guided bombs in the Minicraft F-117 kits in 1/72nd scale and add only the guidance sections. The wing sections, although not entirely correct, will be close enough for most modelers. In 1/32nd scale, the only way to go is to scratchbuild the bombs using a Mk 84 bomb body to start with. Drawings of the GBU-27 are on page 49.

### GBU-27A Paveway III

These bombs are available in 1/144th scale in DML kit 9904 of the F-117A. In all other scales they will have to be built from scratch. This should be one of the easier guided bombs to build from scratch since all of the shapes are relatively simple to make. Scale drawings for this version of the GBU-27 are also on page 49.

### GBU-28 Paveway III

This new deep penetration bomb is not available in any kit. In 1/144th scale the guidance and tail sections from the GBU-27A from DML's kit 9904 of the F-117A could be used with a scratch-built bomb body which could easily be made from sprue or plastic rod. But remember that this weapon was carried only by the F-111F during the war, and is now also certified on the F-15E. Since there is no model of the F-111F in 1/144th scale, there will be relatively little need for the GBU-28 in this scale.

In the other modeling scales, the GBU-28 will have to be built from scratch. However, like the GBU-27A, the shapes are all simple, so this weapon should be easy to model. See page 49 for scale drawings of the GBU-28.

## ELECTRO-OPTICALLY GUIDED BOMBS

### GBU-15(V)-1

This weapon is available in kit form only in 1/72nd scale. It must be scratchbuilt in 1/144th, 1/48th, and 1/32nd scales, and this would be a real challenge. In 1/144th and 1/48th scales the modeler could start with the body of a GBU-8. This weapon can be found in LS kit number S202 in 1/144th scale and Hasegawa kit number X48-2 in 1/48th scale. From this the fins and wings of the GBU-8 would have to be removed and replaced with new ones for the GBU-15(V)-1 made from thin plastic card. In 1/32nd scale, the modeler could start with a Mk 84 bomb body, but from there he would be on his own.

In 1/72nd scale the GBU-15(V)-1 can be found in Hasegawa kit number X72-2. Drawings of this weapon can be found on page 50.

### AGM-62 Walleye

The Walleye is available in kit form in 1/144th, 1/72nd, and 1/48th scales. However, in each case it is the Walleye I that is represented, and this was not used in Operation Desert Storm. It is relatively simple to modify a Walleye I to a Walleye I ER/DL (Extended Range Data Link) by changing the wings. This version was used during the war. The Walleye I ER/DL has a notch cut out in the rear of the wings as shown in the drawing on page 50. The body of the weapon is the same in either case.

The Walleye II ER/DL, which was also used in the Gulf War, has a different body section at the nose than the Walleye I. It also has larger wings with a bigger cutout at the tips of the trailing edge. The modeler may choose to do an extensive modification to Walleye I glide bombs that are in the kits, or build this weapon from scratch. In 1/32nd scale there is no choice other than to start from scratch, but in the other scales we recommend starting with existing Walleye I models.

In 1/144th scale the Walleye I can be found in LS weapons set S202. In 1/72nd scale it can be found in Hasegawa's weapons set X72-4, and the Testors armament kit 860. In 1/48th scale the Walleye I is provided in Hasegawa kit number X48-2. Drawings of the Walleye I ER/DL and Walleye II ER/DL are on page 50.

## STANDARD BOMBS

### Mk 82 AIR, 500-pound bomb

The Mk 82 AIR is not available in any scale in kit form except in 1/48th scale. In other scales, most experienced modelers will be able to convert standard Mk 82 LDGP bombs to the AIR versions. All that is required is to cut off the standard tail section and replace it with a thicker one with different fins.

The one kit that is available of Mk 82 AIR bombs in 1/48th scale is from P. P. Aeroparts. Their kit number AC405 contains six bombs. The bomb bodies are cast resin, and the fins and end plate are photo-etched metal. For information, write to P. P. Models, Studio 2, 9 Bath Buildings, Montpelier, Bristol, United Kingdom, BS6 5PT. Drawings of the Mk 82 AIR are on page 51.

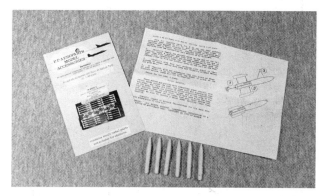

*P. P. Aeroparts produces this excellent kit of Mk 82 AIR bombs in 1/48th scale. The bomb bodies are cast resin, while the fins and rear covers are photoetched metal.*

### Mk 84 AIR, 2000-pound bomb

There are no Mk 84 AIRs in any kit, but the average modeler will be able to convert standard Mk 84 LDGP bombs to the AIR versions by changing the tail section and fins. The Mk 84 in the Testors kit 860 in 1/72nd scale appears to have the AIR tail and fins, but the bomb body is too short. It would be possible to take the AIR tail section off of this bomb and mate it to the Mk 84 bomb in the Hasegawa 1/72nd scale weapons set X72-1, but it would probably be just as simple to build the AIR tail section from scratch. Scale drawings of the Mk 84 AIR are on page 53.

## CLUSTER BOMBS

### Mk 7 CBU dispenser

The Mk 7 dispenser used with the Rockeye series of cluster bombs is available in kit form in three major modeling scales. Although it is not included in the 1/144th scale weapons sets from LS, it is in several aircraft kits. These include the DML kits of the A-6, A-10, and F-15E, among others. In 1/72nd scale, Rockeyes are in Hasegawa's weapons set X72-2 and Testors armament set 860. In 1/48th scale, Rockeyes can be found in Hasegawa's weapons set 48-1. There are no Rockeyes available in kits in 1/32nd scale, so the modeler must scratchbuild the weapon in this scale.

### SUU-30B and -H CBU dispenser

The SUU-30 dispenser, used for the CBU-52, CBU-58, and CBU-71 cluster bombs, is available in 1/144th scale in the LS weapons set S201. It is also in the Hasegawa set S72-2 in 1/72nd scale, but the SUU-30 represented is an SUU-30 or SUU-30A version which had a more pointed nose section and a different fin design. However, modifying this version to the SUU-30B or SUU-30H, as used in the Gulf War, should be a simple task for most modelers. The same thing holds true for the SUU-30s found in Hasegawa weapons set 48-1 in 1/48th scale. We know of no SUU-30 dispensers in any 1/32nd scale kit, so in this scale the dispenser must be built from scratch. Drawings of the SUU-30B and -H are on page 54.

### SUU-64 CBU dispenser

The SUU-64 dispenser is used for the CBU-89. No representations of it exist in kit form, so it must be scratchbuilt by any modeler who wants to display his model with this weapon. Its simple shape should make scratchbuilding it relatively easy. Refer to the drawings on page 55.

### SUU-65 CBU dispenser

The only place the SUU-65 dispenser, which is used with the CBU-87, can be found in kit form is from P. P. Aeroparts. They offer kit number AC719 in 1/72nd scale, and it contains four CBU-87s. However, their advertising calls this a CBU-87 Gator. Gator cluster munitions are CBU-89s and use the SUU-64 dispenser which is very similar in external appearance. They differ only at the aft end where the SUU-65 has an X-shaped plate and the SUU-64 does not. For the address of P.P. Aeroparts, see the section on the Mk 82 AIR bomb.

In all other scales, this weapon must be built from scratch. As in the case of the SUU-64, the simple shape of the SUU-65 should make building this dispenser from scratch an easy task. Drawings of the SUU-65 are on page 55.

## AIR-TO-GROUND MISSILE

### AGM-84E SLAM

There are no models of the Standoff Land Attack Missile available in kit form. However, since the SLAM is a derivative of the AGM-84 Harpoon missile, it is relatively simple to convert models of the Harpoon to the SLAM. Harpoon missiles are available in LS weapons set S202 in 1/144th scale. In 1/72nd scale they can be found in Hasegawa's set X72-4, Testors' kit 860, and Airfix's armament kit 05041. In 1/48th scale they can be obtained from Revell's A-6E kit number 4578. In 1/32nd scale the SLAM must be built from scratch.

All that is necessary to convert the standard Harpoon to the SLAM is to lengthen the missile body a scale twenty inches. This can be done by using two standard Harpoon missiles to make one SLAM. Cut the forward section of one missile off immediately in front of the wings. Cut the second missile off a scale twenty inches in front of the wings. This works out to .14 inches in 1/144th scale, .28 inches in 1/72nd scale, and .42 inches in 1/48th scale. Use the forward section from the first missile and the aft section from the second missile. Join these two parts together, and the result will be an accurate SLAM missile. It will

be helpful if the modeler refers to the drawings of the SLAM that are on page 59.

## ECM PODS

### ALQ-131 shallow ECM pod

There are no models of the ALQ-131 shallow (2 band) ECM pod available, however, it would be simple to convert the several ALQ-131 deep (three band) pods to shallow pods by removing the appropriate lower section. The change that is necessary can be seen in the drawings of the two pods on page 60. ALQ-131 deep pods are available in 1/144th scale in DML kit numbers 4548 and 9908 of the A-10. In 1/72nd scale they can be obtained from Hasegawa weapons set X72-4 and the Italeri F-16C/-D kit number 188. In 1/48th scale they are in Hasegawa weapons set X48-2. Scratchbuilding is the only way to model the ALQ-131 deep or shallow pods in 1/32nd scale.

### ALQ-184 long ECM pod

The ALQ-184 long ECM pod was carried only by 35th TFW F-4G Wild Weasels during Operation Desert Storm. It is externally the same as the ALQ-119 long ECM pod except that it has a longer gondola section as illustrated in the photograph and drawings on page 60. Since no models of the ALQ-184 exist, the simple way to make one is to modify the gondola on one of the many existing ALQ-119 pods that are available in 1/144th to 1/48th scales. The pod would only have to be scratchbuilt in 1/32nd scale if the modeler was doing a conversion of an F-4E to an F-4G in that large scale.

ALQ-119 pods are available in the LS weapons set S202 in 1/144th scale, however, better representations of the pod can be found in DML's kits of the A-10. These are kit numbers 4548 and 9908 in 1/72nd scale, the ALQ-119 is available in Hasegawa's weapons set X72-4 as well as numerous aircraft kits. Hasegawa's set X48-2 contains the ALQ-119, as do several aircraft kits. Following the drawings on page 60, the modeler can convert any of these model ALQ-119 pods to the ALQ-184.

# DESERT STORM DECALS

*General Note: Repli-Scale and Super Scale Decals have released several after-market decal sheets which provide markings used on U.S. combat aircraft that participated in Operation Desert Storm. Many decal sheets issued prior to the war also contain the markings with which the various types of aircraft flew into battle. Because of space limitations, we are primarily listing only those sheets which are marketed specifically as having markings from Desert Shield and Desert Storm for U.S. combat aircraft. In a few instances, when no sheets with Desert Shield or Desert Storm markings are available for a given aircraft, we have listed other sheets that provide the markings which that type of aircraft carried during the Gulf War. A few comments are included when appropriate. This listing is done on an aircraft-by-aircraft basis in the same order that the aircraft are covered in this publication.*

### F-15C Eagle

Repli-Scale provides markings for F-15Cs of the 33rd TFW complete with the kill markings scored in the Gulf War. Sheets 72-1033 and 72-1034 are in 1/72nd scale, and sheets 48-5033 and 48-5034 contain enough markings to build no less than fifteen different aircraft.

Repli-Scale also has a decal sheet for F-15Cs from the 1st TFW during Operation Desert Storm. Included among these is F-15C, 83-017, in which Captain Steve Tate scored a victory on the opening night of the war. Repli-Scale has released these decals in 1/72nd scale on sheet 72-1036 and in 1/48th scale on sheet 48-5036. Additional F-15Cs from the 1st TFW that served in Operation Desert Storm are on Repli-Scale's sheet 72-1037 and 48-5037 in 1/72nd and 1/48th scales respectively. These include the wing commander's aircraft named **Maloney's Pony,** as well as a second aircraft F-15C, 82-023, which bears the same name. The third aircraft is the squadron commander's aircraft for the 27th TFS of the 1st TFW. Markings for three other F-15Cs, 82-010, 83-035, and 83-046, are also provided.

Super Scale also provides markings for F-15Cs from the 1st TFW and the 33rd TFW with Desert Storm kill markings. These decals are available in 1/72nd scale on sheet 72-629, in 1/48th scale on sheet 48-414, and in 1/32nd scale on sheet 32-112. These decals do not appear to be as sharp as those from Repli-Scale, especially when it comes to the name plates for the pilots and crews. Our recommendation is to go with the Repli-Scale sheets.

## F-15E Strike Eagle

There are no after-market decals for the F-15E Strike Eagle with Desert Storm markings. However, since only the 4th TFW (now the 4th Wing) was operational as a combat unit equipped with F-15Es during Operation Desert Storm, previous sheets with their markings can be used. These sheets provide the same markings that were on the Strike Eagles during the war. Repli-Scale's F-15E decal sheets are 1022 in 1/72nd scale, 5022 in 1/48th scale, and 32-02 in 1/32nd scale. These sheets include markings for the wing commander's aircraft. Super Scale's sheets 72-617, 48-401, and 32-101 have F-15E markings in 1/72nd, 1/48th, and 1/32nd scales respectively.

## F-16 Fighting Falcon

Super Scale has released decals for F-16s in Desert Storm markings on sheets in 1/72nd, 1/48th, and 1/32nd scales. These are numbered 72-622, 48-406, and 32-106 respectively. On the 1/72nd and 1/48th scale sheets, markings are provided for an F-16 from the 159th FIS of the Florida Air National Guard. This unit did not participate in Operation Desert Storm. The three other units represented are the 50th TFW, 363rd TFW, and the 421st TFW, all of which flew missions in the Gulf War.

Super Scale sheet 72-608 has 1/72nd scale markings for F-16As from the South Carolina and New York Air National Guards. The markings are the ones that these two units carried during the war, and they are also available in 1/48th scale on sheet 48-368. The New York ANG markings can be found on sheet 32-95 in 1/32nd scale.

## F-4G Wild Weasel

Super Scale sheet 72-660 has 1/72nd scale markings for F-4Gs from both the 35th TFW and the 52nd TFW. These were the two units that flew the Wild Weasels during Operation Desert Storm. The aircraft from the 52nd TFW has mission markings in the form of the famous Phantom "spook" character on the left inlet ramp. Nose art of a charging rhino and the name **Night Stalker** are also carried on this aircraft. These markings are available in 1/48th scale on sheet 48-446. Both sheets also provide markings for an F-4E from the 35th TFW, but this aircraft was not involved in the war.

## RF-4C Phantom II

Repli-Scale has released decals for RF-4Cs in both 1/72nd and 1/48th scales. The 1/72nd scale sheet is 72-1031, and the 1/48th scale sheet is number 48-5031. These each provide markings for six aircraft, three of which have markings used in Desert Shield and Desert Storm. These aircraft are from the 106th TRS of the Alabama Air National Guard, and 66-843 is the squadron commander's aircraft. We used these markings on the Hasegawa RF-4C and discovered some problems. The sharksmouth did not fit, but with some cutting and repositioning of the forward part of the mouth, we got it to work. The gray for the serial number is too light, so it cannot be seen against the gray background of the tail. The instructions state that the trim line next to the anti-glare panel is black. It is 36118 Gunship Gray instead. Regardless of what color it is, it should have been provided as a decal, but it was not. This particular aircraft was photographed extensively by the author shortly after it returned from the Middle East, and it carries a cartoon character of a Confederate soldier and the words "Recce Rebels." Two photographs of some of its markings appear on page 15. Otherwise, this decal sheet is excellent. The other Desert Shield aircraft are "Smooth Charac-

ter," RF-4C, 64-043, and an unnamed RF-4C, 64-044.

Super Scale released sheet 72-659 in 1/72nd scale with markings for three RF-4Cs that participated in Operations Desert Shield and Desert Storm. One is from the Nevada Air National Guard's 192nd TRS, but the markings are pre-Gulf War service. The second aircraft is RF-4C, 69-370, from the 26th TRW. The markings provided are those carried by the aircraft while it was based in Turkey during the war. The third aircraft is from the 67th TRW, and its markings are post-war markings after the wing was redesignated the 67th Reconnaissance Wing (dropping the word "Tactical"). These markings are also on sheet 48-445 in 1/48th scale.

## F-111E and F-111F Aardvark

No after-market decals are available for the F-111E or F-111F with Desert Storm markings. However, other sheets contain unit markings for the 20th TFW's F-111Es and the 48th TFW's F-111F. These are also included in kits. Hopefully, a new sheet will be issued with some of the special mission markings carried by 48th TFW aircraft during the war.

## EF-111A Raven

No after-market decal sheets are available for the EF-111A with Desert Storm markings. However, previous sheets contain unit markings for the 366th TFW and the 42nd ECS. These are also available in kits.

## F-117A Nighthawk

No after-market decals have been released with Desert Storm markings for the F-117A. However, since only the 37th TFW operated the Nighthawk, the available kits and other after-market decal sheets provide the necessary unit insignia. To date, Desert Storm mission markings appear only on decals in the DML 1/144th scale kit 9904, Minicraft's 1/72nd scale kit 2107, Revell's 1/72nd scale kit number 4460, and the Monogram's kit 5834 in 1/48th scale.

## F-14 Tomcat

Super Scale has released several decal sheets with markings used on F-14 Tomcats during Operations Desert Shield and Desert Storm. Sheet 72-620 provides markings in 1/72nd scale for a CAG Tomcat from VF-21 and Carrier Air Wing Fourteen aboard the USS INDEPENDENCE. These markings are also available in 1/48th scale on sheet 48-040 and in 1/32nd scale on sheet 32-104. VF-32 and VF-14 from Carrier Air Wing Three and the USS JOHN F. KENNEDY are also available in 1/72nd and 1/48th scales. The 1/72nd scale sheet is 72-627, and the 1/48th scale sheet is number 48-412. Only the VF-32 aircraft is included in 1/32nd scale, and it is on sheet 32-110.

VF-154 flew from the USS INDEPENDENCE during Desert Shield, and its markings are included on sheet 72-628 in 1/72nd scale. Also on this sheet the modeler will find the markings for VF-74 which flew from the USS SARATOGA during both Desert Shield and Desert Storm. These same two units are also on sheet 48-413 in 1/48th scale. Only the VF-154 aircraft is available in 1/32nd scale on sheet 32-111.

Markings for the two Tomcat squadrons that operated from the USS THEODORE ROOSEVELT during the war are provided on Super Scale sheet 72-650 in 1/72nd scale. These squadrons are VF-41 and VF-84. Both aircraft have "girlie" nose art that was carried during the war. These markings are available in 1/48th scale on sheet 48-438. In 1/32nd scale, the VF-41 aircraft is on sheet 32-122, and the VF-84 aircraft is on sheet 32-123.

### F/A-18 Hornet

More after-market decals have been released for the Hornet than any other aircraft that participated in Operation Desert Storm. Repli-Scale provides markings for three aircraft from VFA-81, including the two F/A-18 Hornets that downed the MiG-21s. The third aircraft is the one in which LCDR Scott Speicher lost his life when it was shot down on the opening night of the war. Sheet 72-1032 provides these markings in 1/72nd scale, and they are also available in 1/48th scale on sheet 48-5032. We have used the 1/72nd scale sheet, and it is excellent.

Repli-Scale also provides markings for F/A-18D Hornets from VMFA-121 which participated in Desert Storm. Other F/A-18Ds from VMFA-242 and VMFAT-101 are also included, however, these units did not participate in the Gulf War. The markings are available on sheet 72-1038 in 1/72nd scale and 48-5038 in 1/48th scale.

A third set of F/A-18 markings from Repli-Scale includes markings for three other Marine Hornet squadrons. These are VMFA-314, VMFA-323, and VMFA-531. Of these, only VMFA-314 flew missions during Operation Desert Storm. The markings are available in 1/72nd scale on sheet 72-1040 and in 1/48th scale on sheet 48-5040.

Super Scale also has decals for Navy F/A-18 Hornets which participated in Operations Desert Shield and Desert Storm. Sheets 72-620 and 72-632 are in 1/72nd scale. The first of these provides markings for a CAG aircraft from VFA-25 of Carrier Air Wing Fourteen which flew from the USS INDEPENDENCE during Desert Shield. The second sheet provides markings for one of the MiG killers of VFA-81. Marine Corps squadron VFMA-451 is also represented in the markings it used during the Gulf War. The fourth aircraft is from VFA-146 and the USS NIMITZ, however, that squadron did not participate in the conflict. The markings on sheet 72-620 are repeated on 48-404 in 1/48th scale and on sheet 48-417, but only the VFMA-451 aircraft is on sheet 32-114 in 1/32nd scale.

More Marine Hornets squadrons are included on Super Scale sheet 72-651 in 1/72nd scale, and these include VMFA-121, VMFA-242, and VMFAT-101. Of these, only VMFA-121 participated in the war. These markings are available in 1/48th scale on sheet 48-439.

### A-6E Intruder

Both Marine A-6E squadrons that participated in Operation Desert Storm are on Super Scale's sheet 72-631 in 1/72nd scale. These are VMA-224 and VMA-533. Also on this sheet are Intruders from VA-85 and VA-115. All four aircraft are also on sheet 48-416 in 1/48th scale.

Super Scale sheet 72-620 provides 1/72nd scale markings for a CAG A-6E from VA-196 and Carrier Air Wing Fourteen. This unit operated from USS INDEPENDENCE during Operation Desert Shield. The same Intruder is also included on decal sheet 48-404 in 1/48th scale.

### EA-6B Prowler

Markings for three EA-6B Prowlers that saw action in Operation Desert Storm are provided in 1/72nd scale on Super Scale sheet 72-648. The same decals are also available in 1/48th scale on sheet 48-436. The aircraft are from VAQ-131 and the USS RANGER, VAQ-141 and the USS THEODORE ROOSEVELT, and VAQ-137 and the USS AMERICA. The VAQ-141 aircraft is particularly interesting with its nose art that depicts a bikini-clad lady riding a HARM anti-radiation missile. She is called **DECEPTION LASS** and is named **EVE OF DESTRUCTION.**

Super Scale sheet 72-620 also provides markings for a Prowler from VAQ-139 and Carrier Air Wing Fourteen from the USS INDEPENDENCE. This CAG aircraft participated in Operation Desert Shield. The same markings are provided in 1/48th scale on sheet 48-404.

### A-7E Corsair II

Markings for the A-7's last cruise are available from Super Scale on sheet 72-626 in 1/72nd scale and 48-411 in 1/48th scale. This last cruise saw the Corsair's participation in Operations Desert Shield and Desert Storm when the Navy's last two A-7 squadrons flew from the deck of the USS JOHN F. KENNEDY. Markings from both VA-72 and VA-46 are provided, and these include the specially marked aircraft shown on the front cover of this book. Unfortunately, the markings for this Corsair are incomplete in that the names are missing from the exhaust cone. It should also be noted that this aircraft was painted in its special markings only after the hostilities were over and the KENNEDY was heading home. Also provided on these sheets are markings for another aircraft from VA-46 as well as the squadron commander's aircraft from VA-72. Both of these Corsairs are in the standard tactical paint scheme and have numerous mission markers on the nose.

### AV-8B Harrier II

Super Scale sheet 72-625 has markings in 1/72nd scale for AV-8B Harriers from four different units. Of these, VMA-231 (misidentified as VMAT-231 in the name of the sheet) saw action in the Gulf War and had Desert Storm markings on the nose of its aircraft. These markings were in the form of a bomb with the number of missions flown written on it. **FREE KUWAIT** was written above the bomb in Arabic. Markings for two Harriers from this unit are provided on this sheet. The same markings are also available in 1/48th scale on sheet 48-410, where the unit is again misidentified as VMAT-231. The other three AV-8B squadrons covered by these sheets did not participate in Operation Desert Storm.

### A-10 Warthog

Decal sheets 72-644 and 72-645 from Super Scale provide markings for A-10s, some of which were used in Desert Storm. Sheet 72-644 contains markings for Warthogs from the 354th TFW and the 23rd TFW. Both of these units saw action in the Gulf War, and these aircraft each have Desert Storm mission markings painted on the fuselage. The aircraft from the 354th TFW is named **HOG 1,** and the one from the 23rd TFW is named **#1 TANK KILLER.** The other A-10 on the sheet is from the 917th TFW, and it is in a special gray scheme. This unit and this aircraft did not participate in Operation Desert Storm. The markings on sheet 72-644 are also available on sheet 48-432 in 1/48th scale.

Sheet 72-645 has markings for A-10s from the 23rd TASS and the 10th TFW, both of which flew missions in the war. The aircraft from the 23rd TASS is named **Live and Let Die,** and has mission markers on the right side of the nose. The A-10 from the 10th TFW has mission markers on the left side of the fuselage, and it is named **Have Gun Will Travel.** An A-10 in a tan and brown scheme from the 917th TFW is also included, but it did not participate in Desert Storm. These markings are also available in 1/48th scale on sheet 48-433.

### B-52G Stratofortress

Since the only kits of the B-52G that are available are in 1/144th and 1/200th scales, no after-market decals are available. It has been several years since any decal companies produced sheets for kits smaller than 1/72nd scale.